fun·da·men·tal-*ish*

Jeff Farnham

Jer 32:17

fun·da·men·tal-*ish*

adjective

1. how compromise under the guise of relevance blurs the lines between fundamentalists and evangelicals.

SWORD OF THE LORD

P. O. Box 1099 • Murfreesboro, TN 37133
swordofthelord.com

contents

dedication

To Shelton and Betty Smith
My first pastor and pastor's wife,
Who welcomed me into their home and lives,
Who introduced me to independent
Baptist fundamentalism,
Who helped me comprehend God's call to ministry,
Who afforded me my first opportunity to preach in church,
And who have supported my wife and me for over
four decades

To David and Pat Lawrence
My first youth pastor and youth pastor's wife,
Who welcomed me into their family and inner circle,
Who showed compassion and understanding,
Who insisted on my giving my testimony in youth group,
Who introduced me to beautiful Christian music,
And who whetted my appetite to reach others

foreword

Pagan invasions against long-held precious Christian beliefs of God's people have become headline issues in twenty-first-century, independent Baptist fundamentalism. Like the staunch defenders of the faith in the previous century, separated saints stand strong and stalwart against these spiritual, moral, and civil encroachments. Hats off to every godly man and woman in our day who defends the faith of the Scripture and the faithful of the land.

Seemingly less harmful—and as a result more tolerable—are the cultural invasions against time-honored precious Christian beliefs of God's people. Just as Babylonian and Medo-Persian culture tainted all but the godliest of the Jews during the Captivity, so Western culture has diluted the purity of an appreciable population of the saints in our nation.

In the latter half of the twentieth century, it was not uncommon for a church to call itself baptistic but not Baptist. In this new millennium, the westernization of Christianity has spawned a fundamental-ish crowd that is not truly fundamental, even as baptistic churches are not honestly Baptist.

During the last three decades of the twentieth century, independent fundamental Baptists lost vast numbers to the neo-evangelical church movement. In this new century, neo-evangelicalism has gone off the rails so far that independent Baptists have little appetite for it. Instead, independent fundamental Baptist churches are losing members to a different group. Relevance, the most attractive and effective mask that compromise has ever worn, is siphoning independent fundamental Baptists into fundamental-ish churches.

Fundamental-ish brethren contend for a fundamental-ish faith, practice fundamental-ish liberties, sing and perform fundamental-ish music, wear fundamental-ish attire, learn fundamental-ish ideas, participate in fundamental-ish dialogue, organize fundamental-ish conferences, engage in fundamental-ish pastimes, embrace fundamental-ish standards, and attend—and even pastor—fundamental-ish churches.

Necessary to the spiritual success of our churches and families in this culture is a repentance regarding fundamental-ish adaptations to culture. Additionally, said spiritual success in our churches and families requires the return to absolute compliance with the written Word of God, absolute alliance with Christ the head of the church, and absolute reliance upon the Holy Spirit of God for power and victory.

May God use this book to call fundamental-ish brethren back to the historical independent Baptist fundamentalism of godly separation and holy living.

Jeff Farnham
LaGrange, Indiana
June 2019

chapter one

Fundamentalist Five-Pointers

Reasons for Fundamental-ish Thinking

When the movement still known as fundamentalism gained its identity and its impetus in the 1930s as a backlash against 1920s German rationalism and Darwinian unbelief that was infiltrating American seminaries and pulpits, five absolutely necessary beliefs or fundamentals were established:

(1) inspiration and preservation of Scripture

(2) the deity of Jesus Christ

(3) the virgin birth and humanity of Jesus Christ

(4) the blood atonement of Jesus Christ

(5) the bodily resurrection of Jesus Christ

The unwritten sixth fundamental was separation from those who did not believe the previous five. Those of any denominational attachment who subscribed to, accepted and believed these five fundamentals, and furthermore, were willing to stand against those who rejected those five fundamentals, became known as fundamentalists.

In order to properly understand the religious climate under which this multi-denominational conglomerate laid aside its differences to establish fundamentalism and wage war against modernism and liberalism, it must be remembered that in the 1930s, a majority of Americans were church-attending believers in the Savior, Jesus Christ. Even mainline denominations that were engaging in dialogue with apostasy still had among their ranks appreciable majorities of church members who were trusting in Christ for the forgiveness of sin and for their eternity in Heaven. For that reason, and perhaps others, the founders of the fundamentalist movement did not seek to separate from entire denominations, but only from those within the denominations who embraced—or at least entertained—the denial of the five fundamentals, and who in turn, would not separate from others who also entertained and embraced such denial.

That being said, the 1930s and 1940s and 1950s saw a yoking up and a cooperation of fundamentalists (those who embraced the five fundamentals and separated from those who did not) from among the Baptists along with many from among the Methodists, Presbyterians, Assemblies of God, Pentecostals and other denominations that had developed at different times in history since the Protestant Reformation. The particulars of baptism, communion, church polity and pastoral leadership were set aside, as long as the individual or church remained loyal to the five fundamentals and separated from those who reneged on that loyalty. Cooperation amongst those who "defended the faith" led to great city-wide campaigns and God did work via those post-depression-era, World-War-II-era efforts.

Somewhat contemporary in time with this banding together of fundamentalists from among the Baptists and from within many denominational groups was a growing unrest concerning the unwritten sixth fundamental: separation. If one is to understand fundamentalism as a movement and fundamentalists as people, he must comprehend the scriptural precept, position and practice of separation.

Separation served as the catalyst to conceive, birth and grow the movement known as fundamentalism. So connected to separation is the fundamentalist movement that it would be accurate to state that fundamentalism was cultured in a petri dish of separation. It would be equally honest to say that without separation there would be no fundamentalist movement among believers.

By the mid-1950s, the previously mentioned unrest with the separatists had reached a fevered pitch. An equally fervent group of men and women and churches began to promote the idea that the five fundamentals were right but that the unwritten sixth fundamental of separation was too militant, too stringent, too exclusive, too incompatible with God's love—indeed, too unnecessary. These people wanted to occupy theological turf between the fundamentalists and the modernists, between the Bible-believers and the Bible-belittlers, between the staunch supporters of Scripture and the equally determined detractors from doctrine. So famous became their rallying cry that one fundamentalist published a pamphlet about them entitled *The In-Betweenites,* a takeoff from James Henley Thornwell's nineteenth-century name for those even in his day who said they loved truth but were soft in their stance and refused to boldly withstand error. Calling themselves New (Neo-) Evangelicals and their movement New (Neo-) Evangelicalism, they fervently followed this middle-of-the-road ideology.

Again, history will bring understanding. New Evangelicals did not react to the fundamentalists over any of the five fundamentals; rather, they reacted to fundamentalists' adherence to separation. They did not want to be separatists. They wanted to believe in the five fundamentals but do so with "compassion" and "understanding" of an American church population that was rapidly embracing a sympathy toward the questioning of the Bible and progressively developing a tolerance of disbelief of Scripture. In the same way that fundamentalism was a backlash against modernism, New Evangelicalism was a backlash against that backlash.

In summary, then, one must see that the entire history of fundamentalism is vested in separation. Without separation there would be no fundamentalist movement (and perhaps no Neo-Evangelical movement). It is just as true that without separation in our day, there is no fundamentalism.

Fast forward seventy years from the establishment of the New Evangelical movement, and the vast majority of the United States citizenry is now apostate, largely due to belief systems ranging all the way from New Evangelicalism to tolerant paganism to radical atheism. However, fundamentalism that defines itself by the five fundamentals agreed upon seventy years ago (when the spiritual climate of our nation was completely different) is still somewhat intact.

Many twenty-first-century independent Baptist fundamentalists have comforted themselves into thinking that their holding to the five fundamentals is still sufficient, either inadvertently forgetting or purposely neglecting to realize that the spiritual climate in the twenty-first century is quite different than that of the 1930s, 1940s, and 1950s. They quite resemble soldiers who are still fighting as if the geography and weaponry of the world were what they were in the First World War. They have missed the fact that battle fronts, battle lines, battle issues and battle armories have changed. They have ignored the obvious facts that many nations that existed then no longer do, that nations existing now did not exist then, that national borderlines have changed, that alliances are different and that World War One weaponry is far outdated by the technologically-advanced arsenals of today.

When fundamentalists announced their five fundamentals in the 1930s, there was no battle for the King James Bible against a hundred other versions because those hundred other Bible versions had not been published. No battle for modesty was being waged because all decent people (even most unsaved, unchurched people) covered up in chaste, gender-distinct, appropriate clothing. No skirmishes against rock music were being fought because there was no rock music, to say nothing of its churchy cousin, Christian rock. No one was needing to position himself with regard to R-rated (or worse) media because there was no such thing.

No churches had to take up sword and shield against anti-God, anti-Bible, anti-Creation secular education, because the public education system still embraced the reading of the Bible and prayer in school classrooms. No believers had to establish their ground concerning non- and inter-denominationalism because no one had ever heard of such movements, nor had anyone but the rankest of left-wingers even envisioned that such movements would or could ever exist in "Christian America."

The hyphenated adjective *five-point* is familiarly ascribed to Calvinism and Calvinists; however, employment of that descriptor for fundamentalism or fundamentalists is rare. Rare, but necessary. In this radically-changing twenty-first-century, there exist individuals and churches among fundamentalism that hold to five points of cardinal doctrine but neglect to maintain the separatist stand that is identified with historic independent Baptist fundamentalism.

Fundamentalists who are saying in essence that all one needs in this new millennium are the five fundamentals of original fundamentalism from the 1930s are deserving of the monikers "five-point fundamentalism" (the position) and "five-point fundamentalist" (the persons holding the position). Incredible though it may sound, an earthquake and its resulting tsunami of this position are occurring. An increasingly large segment of "American fundamentalism" is retreating on one or more important matters of separation, comforting itself that it still believes in the inspiration and preservation of Scripture, the deity of Jesus Christ, the virgin birth and humanity of Jesus Christ, the blood atonement of Jesus Christ, and bodily resurrection of Jesus Christ.

These five-point fundamentalists hold to the five fundamentals that one must believe and receive in order to be saved, while they abandon separation from one or more damaging worldly trends that will hinder their impact for Jesus Christ. Indeed, they are bold and decisive regarding terminology but conciliatory and neutral concerning practicality. These believers still fly their banners with the words *Baptist* and *independent* and *fundamentalist* in bold capital letters, but they leaven those very words by sheathing the Sword of the Spirit on contemporary issues. They remain verbally loyal to terms like *blood-bought* and soul-conscious, yet they breach their own work with turncoat cowardice when they face the need to separate from modern devices of worldliness. As a result they become less fundamental and lean towards being fundamental-ish.

The need of this hour is a keeping of biblical, historic, independent Baptist positions along with an establishing of biblical positions on issues which have come to be in the present century. Such an expanded position must now include far more than those five noble fundamentals agreed upon in a necessary reaction to unbelief that occurred nearly a century ago. While those five fundamentals may still be viewed as a minimal set of criteria for salvation, fellowship and cooperation must be based upon far more. Those five precious fundamentals are agreeably the necessities for the faith of a child of a God. However, walking together with another brother in a world of Noahic atrocities and Sodomite abominations and Lot-like abasements involves much more.

Lest one read this and conceive that the cry for separation not only from apostasy but also from compromise is new, let that one read the prophet Hosea who said, "Ephraim, he hath mixed himself among the people..." (Hos. 7:8). This is a lamentation by the first of the minor prophets, as he discovered the belligerent, brazen position of Israel in the middle of the eighth century B.C.

Truthfully, all of Hosea chapter seven depicts a scenario of independent Baptist fundamentalists who want to stick to the five points but they go to Egypt (the world) and Assyria (the flesh) for their model, music, mentorship, methods or modesty. Continuing to put to the record God's obvious displeasure with Israel's yoking with unbelief, Hosea wrote that Israel was "bent to backsliding...though they called them to the most High, none at all would exalt him...Ephraim feedeth on wind, and followed after the east wind: he daily increaseth lies and desolation; and they do make a covenant with the Assyrians, and oil is carried into Egypt" (Hos.11:7, 12:1). To be "bent" toward backsliding means to have a tendency or a leaning toward backsliding. Indeed, five-point fundamentalism has that propensity.

Also consider the prophet Amos who asked, "Can two walk together, except they be agreed?" (Amos 3:3). Walking together is much more than salvation; it is sanctification and surrender and service and solutions and serenity. Walking together is far more than eternal life; it is one's love and lowliness and liberty and Lamb-likeness. In context, Amos was asking the people of the northern kingdom of Ephraim if they thought God could walk with them in their spiritual idolatries and iniquities. The answer to this rhetorical question is a "No" that would echo from Calvary to the rapture. Because all Scripture is God-inspired and therefore profitable for all, the Holy Spirit still asks this question today and the answer is the same. God can most definitely not walk with any man who pursues idolatry. While most Americans have not carved gods out of wood or stone, a large percentage of Americans calling themselves Christians have carved a god out of secular ideas. Again, God can most definitely not walk with any man who tolerates, or worse, pursues, the iniquity of compromise.

By further application the Holy Spirit asks the man who walks with God if he can walk side-by-side and heart-to-heart with another man who walks apart from God. Again, the answer remains a decided "No." One who is a biblical Christian and allows the Christ of Christianity to sanctify his life cannot walk together with one who is saved but refuses the sanctifying work of that same Christ in his life.

This is not to confuse the matter of what is often termed progressive sanctification. Believers in the Lord Jesus Christ find themselves at different places along the pathway to Glory. The journey from the cross to the crown is populated by people who have just entered at the gate of faith, others who have traveled a short way, and others who have traveled many miles. By the grace of God each pilgrim is at the place where he is. The key is that sanctification is moving, not stationary. By its very definition walking together involves motion, and two can walk together only if they are both progressing.

Failure to achieve a particular step in sanctification is not the equivalent of failure to activate the will and move toward that particular step. Not knowing what is expected is not equal to knowing but not doing what is expected. Walking together is the subject of Amos' question. It is also the subject of one of Paul's questions. Comparing Titus to himself, he asked, "Walked we not in the same spirit? walked we not in the same steps?" (II Cor. 12:18).

Again, just as sanctification and walking together possess interactive quality, so do service and walking together. By *service* is meant the actual service of God. Malachi, another Old Testament prophet of fundamentalist separatism, called for a discerning "between the righteous and the wicked, between him that serveth God and him that serveth him not" (Mal. 3:18).

Many who are "busy for God" are not serving Him; others who are "paid to serve God," positioned within high places in prominent churches, are not serving Him. One must carefully discern between those who are serving God and those who are serving "camps" and colleges, isms and schisms, popes and power.

dialogue of walking together

When two individuals are walking together, they have dialogue; that is, they converse. The subjects vary widely depending upon the walkers' concerns, responsibilities and preferences. However, they talk. It would rare be to hear that one had taken a walk with someone else, but that neither had spoken a word. Furthermore, it would be uncommon to hear that two had taken a walk together, but that neither had talked about anything of importance or of interest to the other. Indeed, were such a twosome to walk together, they would soon be bored of each other and find different walking companions.

When spiritual matters are of importance and interest to two individuals, they want to converse about them. When two separate persons agree and have similar outlooks on a number of spiritual subjects, they can have rewarding fellowship. Such rewarding fellowship promotes further walks and talks. However, if the two see those same spiritual matters from such different perspectives as to mutually exclude each other's ideas and insights, the conversation is unpleasant, unrewarding, even disturbing. Eventually, if not immediately, the two stop walking together because the dialogue is abrasive to each. Rather than being iron sharpening iron, they find that one of them is the fingernail and the other is the chalkboard, and that the screech brings a shudder to them both.

devotion of walking together

Two who are walking together give attention to stay at the same pace so that one does not leave the other behind. They walk at the same pace and maintain the same speed. When one walks, the other walks. When one increases speed, so does the other. When the pace of one slows, the pace of the other does as well. When one rests, the other rests. The two are devoted one to the other.

Observe the walkers in any given town. Down the sidewalk comes a young couple, power-walking, arms swinging and weights dangling. They are mutually devoted to health and fitness. Side by side, they keep pace.

Across the street are two aged men. They have known each other for decades and they are heading to their favorite breakfast restaurant. Notice how they walk beside each other, and if one of them is healthier than the other, the healthy one does not stroll into the restaurant and leave his feebler friend to shuffle in later.

No. The robust man devotedly takes his friend's arm and helps him along. The faster man is slowed down somewhat, but the weaker man is helped along so that they both arrive at the same time.

Go to the park in your town and watch a mother with her toddler. She can walk at three or four miles per hour, but her devotion to that sweet child slows her down. She takes tiny steps matching the speed of her precious one.

What would happen if one of those fitness-conscious souls suddenly became intensely competitive or if that palsied older gentleman became upset at his friend's help? What would occur if that mother got frustrated with her child's inability to keep up? In all these scenarios the twosomes would become lonesome "onesomes" and the walking together would cease.

As two spiritual people walk along, they demonstrate devotion to each other. The speed at which they progress is often determined by the person with the lesser understanding of spiritual matters. The more mature believer "slows down" to accommodate the untaught one. However, if one refuses to adjust to help another, or if one denies the help, the walking together is done.

dependence of walking together

When two are walking together, they depend upon each other for encouragement, interest, and purpose. Usually, walkers are in pairs or groups, or if it is one person, he often has a leashed dog along for exercise. Man is dependent by nature, resting upon the companionship and camaraderie of another for each step of his trek. Few demanding exercises in life last long unless the one maintaining the calisthenics routine has a supportive, faithful partner. Indeed,

"Two are better than one; because they have a good reward for their labour.

"For if they fall, the one will lift up his fellow: but woe to him that is alone when he falleth; for he hath not another to help him up."—Eccles. 4:9, 10.

In the realm of spiritual fellowship and walking together, Pauls depend upon Timothys and Timothys depend upon Pauls. "Each for the other and both for the Lord" is a slogan of true dependence manifested by biblical pairs who walked together in dependence in both Testaments: Job and Abraham, Israel and Joseph, Joshua and Caleb, Barak and Deborah, David and Jonathan, Elijah and Elisha, Isaiah and Hosea, Isaiah and Hezekiah, Jeremiah and Baruch, Jeremiah and Josiah, Jesus Christ and John, Paul and Silas, Paul and Timothy, and John and Gaius. Just as truly, biblical pairs who did not maintain healthy two-way dependence ceased to walk together: Abraham and Lot, Isaac and Ishmael, Jacob and Laban, Samuel and Saul, David and Joab, Paul and Demas, John and those who "went out" (I John 2:19) and Demetrius and Diotrophes.

direction of walking together

Again, walking together involves direction. A man walking west will find it impossible to be together with a man walking east. They will meet, but they will not walk together. They are traveling in opposite directions. Even directions that are not diametric opposites present difficulty and impossibility to the concept of walking together. What if one is traveling north-northwest and the other is traveling northwest? These two compass points are side by side, and for a short time, the two will be close enough to be defined as walking together. However, with the passage of time, even slightly different direction renders walking together impossible.

The east and west travelers illustrate the lost and the saved who are traveling in completely incompatible directions. The north-northwest traveler and the northwest portrays two believers progressing in directions that soon prevent their walking together. The unspiritual believer who is traveling with the world is not traveling in the same direction as the spiritual believer who is walking with God. The carnal believer whose life is consumed with self is hardly moving in a direction identical with a spiritual believer whose life is prioritized by the Savior. For two to walk together, they must be making headway in an identical direction.

distance of walking together

Again, walking together implies distance. If a man takes only two steps beside another man, it is unlikely to be called walking together. However, if someone goes a mile with another soul, he can say he has walked together with that one. Married couples who remain faithful walk together for ten, twenty-five or perhaps fifty years. Two businessmen engaged in the same work may walk together for decades.

In the spiritual context walking together for the distance involves an agreement that produces distance. If two believers agree on the subject of abortion, but disagree on everything else, they will not walk far together. However, if they believe the same on thirty or forty major issues ranging from God to the church to the family to society in general, they can walk together for a long journey. They will stay near each other because of the nearness of their positions.

destination of walking together

Finally, when two walk together, they are moving toward the

same destination. When two separate individuals determine by the grace of God to end up closer to Jesus by day's end, they can walk together because their destination is Jesus. Indeed, they are the ones who are "looking unto Jesus" (Heb. 12:2) and "press[ing] toward the mark" (Phil. 3:14).

While it is true that biblical Christians and compromising Christians are all going to end up in Heaven, the destinations along the journey are quite different. When the biblical Christian is headed for church on Sunday night, the compromiser is headed to the ball game. When the biblical Christian is driving to a prayer meeting or a revival meeting, the pragmatic saint is driving to the mall. When the biblical Christian is walking into the prayer closet, the "free believer" is walking to the park. When the biblical Christian is making plans around his God, the excuse-maker is bending his god around his plans. When the biblical Christian is seeking the fullness of the Holy Spirit so that the Christ-life may be lived out in reality in his body, the carnal churchgoer is seeking popularity and position so that he can live unto himself. The daily destinations are not the same.

How precious it is, then, when two believers can walk together because they have sweet and amenable dialogue, experiencing the fulfillment of God's promises, respecting His statutes, delighting in His commandments, observing His laws, growing wiser through His testimonies and submitting to His judgments. How beautiful it is to see two saints who can walk together because of their selfless, God-glorifying devotion to one another. How lovely it is that two children of God can walk together in spiritually wholesome dependence with each voluntarily giving good to the other. How good it is to see two of the sons of God who can walk together in the same direction, going the distance and arriving at the same destination in an unbroken fellowship of truth and faith.

detriments to walking together

Several detriments to walking together have already been noted in previous paragraphs. In reading this, it may strike the casual reader that the author believers that everyone who is not in total agreement with him has embraced five-point fundamentalism. Let it not be that any reader would be that careless. Moreover, let it not be that any reader considers the author to be so. However, we cannot dismiss the importance of serious hindrances to fellowship and walking together that have become hindrances in recent years and decades. Methods, mentorship, music, modesty and ministry model issues of our day have changed and thus become detriments to spiritual fellowship and walking together to the true separatist.

Obvious to any observer is that those who make accommodations to the age and tolerate compromises with the culture do not all start at the same place. In some ministries, music is first to be compromised; in others, it is methods or mentorship or modesty or the ministry model. However, less obvious but tantamount to the issue is that "the beginning of strife is as when one letteth out water" (Prov. 17:14). The beginning of compromise, in whatever area, is like opening a dam from which the waters of other compromises flow. One compromise yields others, and from that initial compromise and its ensuing strife comes the unagreed walk of broken fellowships. Behold the churches of our day who are compromising in only one or two areas mentioned here. Just a decade ago, those churches had not compromised in those areas and a decade from now they will have compromised in two or three more areas. The fundamentalist five-pointers of today are the New Evangelicals of tomorrow! True Baptist fundamentalists, let us shun fundamental-ish leanings and let us become a modern-day band of Shammahs (and stand in the midst of our ground and defend our lentil patch against the Philistines!)

chapter two

How Readest Thou?

Fundamental-ish Liberties

In Luke's account of Jesus' life and ministry, an account is given of a lawyer who stood up to tempt Christ in front of the crowd that our Lord was addressing. His question was this: "Master, what shall I do to inherit eternal life?" (Luke 10:25). Rather than actually answering the critic's question, Jesus Himself asked two questions: "What is written in the law? how readest thou?" (vs. 26)

In English a second question single-spaced from a previous question without its first word's being capitalized is contextually understood to be an extension of the first question. The first question from the lips of our Savior was a question for which the lawyer could give an objective answer as to the exact content of the law. The second question, however, demanded the lawyer give a subjective answer as to his understanding of that content. Jesus was not asking the lawyer how he read in the sense of asking how his eyes coordinated with his brain to transfer a message from the scroll to his thoughts; rather, our Lord was asking the lawyer what message and meaning he took from his reading.

Notably, the lawyer gave the correct answer, citing Deuteronomy 6:5 and Leviticus 19:18. This man, despite his less-than-admirable motive, gave a most admirable answer. He spoke the specific words that comforted his soul to the point that he could think well of himself. He calculatedly and mechanically recited the requirement of the Old Testament Law to love God with all one's heart, soul, strength and mind and also to love one's neighbor as he loved himself. However, he just could not leave well enough alone. In that ubiquitous spirit of proud men, he sought to justify himself by asking Jesus who that neighbor might be.

The lawyer's question about the identity of his neighbor revealed that, while he had read the precise words of the Law about neighbors, he did not correctly understand the meaning of the word *neighbor*. Frankly, this lawyer had actually assigned to the specific word *neighbor* a definition and connotation that made room in his arrogant spirit for him to inwardly possess chagrin and outwardly manifest malice toward some of his fellows. This gave rise to Jesus' utterance of the story commonly known as the parable of the Good Samaritan. The whole purpose of our Lord in recounting the unfortunate events of this traveler from Jerusalem to Jericho was that the lawyer might apply the correct definition to the word *neighbor* which he had correctly spoken but incorrectly understood.

True fundamentalists make every effort to draw their definitions for biblical words from the English meanings written into the 1611 King James Bible.

Those definitions were in place and understood among English-speaking people prior to the 1920s when began the downward evolution of English as a language. Some of these definitions are obvious. Colossians 3:5 defines covetousness as idolatry. Hebrews 11:1 defines faith as "the substance of things hoped for, the evidence of things not seen." Romans 14:17 declares that "the kingdom of God is…righteousness, and peace, and joy in the Holy Ghost." Second John 1:6 says, "And this is love, that we walk after his commandments." Many more such ostentatious definitions written right into the text of God's Word could be cited. Whether the definitions of specific words are given or implied, God-fearing independent Baptist separatists have historically sought to preserve the pure definitions of Bible words.

The purity and beauty of English as a viable mode of expression was unrivaled prior to the onset of theological liberalism in the early 1900s. Progressively, since the decades when German rationalism and higher criticism gained the recognition of Westcott-and-Hort scorners and Pecksniffian scholars, the English language has suffered insidious damage due to arrogant intellectualism and ignorant socio-redefining. Word definitions, consequently, have evolved, and the general public—Christian or not—uses in each generation the accepted definition of a word more than its biblical definition.

Neo-Evangelical speakers and writers make no pretense about their practice of defining biblical words by social and cultural norms of the modern day. The employment of an altered definition, even if the adjustment is ever so slight, will result in an overall moving of the ancient landmark of that word's former meaning. These definition-changers are not holding fast the form of sound words (II Tim. 1:13) as the Holy Ghost inspired Paul to command to Timothy. Rather, they are altering that form in an effort to bend the Bible around popular culture and belief and lifestyle. This language variation contributes in part to some of the disagreement between present-day independent Baptist fundamentalists and some who yet call themselves fundamentalists but are slowly morphing the historic biblical position into a compromise on points other than the five fundamentals.

Specific to the issue and to the focus of this book and chapter is the comprehension of the general church public of the word *liberty*, and of two closely related words, *charity* and *offense*. The author asks you, the reader, "What is written in the Scripture concerning liberty? how readest thou? What is written in God's Word regarding charity? how readest thou? What is written in the Bible bearing upon offense? how readest thou?"

The King James New Testament employs the word *liberty* eighteen times in seventeen verses to convey five different types of privilege or freedom: civil liberty, soul liberty, personal liberty, eternal liberty and Christian liberty. While it is the last usage that will be discussed here, the other four must also be clearly defined for complete understanding of this all-important matter.

four types of liberty

CIVIL LIBERTY. The first of these types of liberty just listed, civil liberty, is freedom guaranteed by an authorized government as exemplified when Felix "commanded a centurion to keep Paul, and to let him have liberty, and that he should forbid none of his acquaintance to minister or come unto him" (Acts 24:23). Another example of civil liberty was noted when Paul wrote, "Know ye that our brother Timothy is set at liberty" (Heb. 13:23). In both cases, liberty was granted by agents of an earthly government in accord with that government's laws.

God instituted in the theocratic, Mosaic system a year of release every seven years and a year of jubilee every fifty years. Every seventh year, a Hebrew servant was to be released to liberty and "go out free for nothing" (Exod. 21:2). Every fiftieth year, the high priest was to "proclaim liberty throughout all the land unto all the inhabitants thereof" (Lev. 25:10). In both situations this was a civil liberty granted by the priestly leaders of the theocratic government of Israel to the citizens of that called-out nation.

SOUL LIBERTY. The second type of liberty listed earlier and mentioned in Scripture, constitutes the freedom given to the souls of men to choose or reject Christ for salvation, to choose or reject truth for obedience, and to choose or reject principles of Scripture for living. In essence, the Lord Jesus spoke with this liberty in mind when He came to the synagogue in Nazareth. The Bible says,

> "...he found the place where it was written,
>
> "The Spirit of the Lord is upon me, because he hath anointed me to preach the gospel to the poor; he hath sent me to heal the brokenhearted, to preach deliverance to the captives, and recovering of sight to the blind, to set at liberty them that are bruised,
>
> "To preach the acceptable year of the Lord."—Luke 4:17–19.

The preaching of the Gospel to poor, lost sinners has always been for the purpose of healing broken hearts, delivering captive souls, giving sight to blind eyes and giving liberty to oppressed persons. However, neither the prophets nor the apostles nor Jesus Christ Himself—nor biblical Christians of any era for that matter—ever forced faith in that Gospel upon anyone.

The prophets, the apostles, the Lord Jesus and the Christian witness of this century give the message; the hearer has liberty to accept it or reject it. The hearer is not given liberty to determine the consequences of his choice; however, he does have liberty in the choice itself.

No wonder Moses cried out to his generation, "I call Heaven and earth to record this day against you, that I have set before you life and death, blessing and cursing: therefore choose life, that both thou and thy seed may live" (Deut. 30:19).

No wonder Paul had, "great heaviness and continual sorrow in my heart…for my brethren, my kinsmen according to the flesh" (Rom. 4:2-3). No wonder his "heart's desire and prayer to God for Israel is that they might be saved" (10:1). Christian liberty is presented every time the Gospel or some truth of God is proclaimed. Hearers have freedom to hear or not to hear.

PERSONAL LIBERTY. The third kind of liberty addressed in Scripture is personal liberty. It is the roominess and relief one can experience when he is untethered by specific commandment, law or restriction. In certain places and under certain circumstances, God gives an individual freedom to choose in matters of his or her personal life. This is beautifully illustrated in the case of the Christian widow: "The wife is bound by the law as long as her husband liveth; but if her husband be dead, she is at liberty to married to whom she will; only in the Lord" (I Cor. 7:39). This verse says if a woman is single because her husband is dead, she may marry another man but only a saved man. Her personal freedom, however, is in the following words: "She is at liberty to be married to whom she will." In this aspect the widow has an unrestrained release either to remarry or to not remarry. In other words, there is no scriptural authority to say that a widow must or must not remarry; rather, God gives freedom that she may or may not remarry as she chooses. In this specific case within the stated parameters, she is right whether she marries or remains single in her widowhood.

ETERNAL LIBERTY. In the fourth place there is the matter of eternal liberty that will one day be enjoyed by all believers. Romans 8:21 speaks of a future time when all believers "shall be delivered from the bondage of corruption into the glorious liberty of the children of God." This statement is made in a passage about the ultimate deliverance of the soul from all the entrapments of the flesh when Jesus Christ raises the body in its glorified state. In the meantime, "The creature waiteth of the manifestation of the sons of God" and is still "subject to vanity" and yet "groaneth and travaileth" (vss. 19–22). It is in this state of unglorified vanity and travail that even the best of believers must live. Ironically, it is in full recognition of this state of corruption that our Lord Jesus Christ expects believers to live out the last type of liberty in the aforementioned list, Christian liberty. One Old Testament reference, along with most of the New Testament references to the word *liberty*, speak of Christian liberty, a deliverance in which the saints of God enjoy particular favors and freedoms from their Heavenly Father as provided within the scope of scriptural truth.

As stated earlier, the mis-defining and misunderstanding of a given word leads to the misapplication of that word. In other words, an improper creed leads to improper conduct. The balance of this chapter will show that Christian liberty, properly understood, leads to Christian liberty properly lived. At the same time, this chapter will demonstrate that (1) what many believe to be matters of soul liberty and/or personal liberty are actually issues of Christian liberty, and (2) what many compromising fundamentalists call their Christian liberty is actually licentiousness under the auspices of a local church.

the proper view of liberty

The licentious view of Christian liberty gives far too much credibility to what are commonly and conveniently called *gray areas* and far too little respect to God's desires, stated or implied, on the matters of life. The more a person believes that God has spoken to every area of life, the more he understands that the

Lord has declared His clear position and demanded believers' consecrated practice for every area of life. The less a person believes that God has spoken to all the needs of mankind, the more likely he is to develop a longer and longer list of supposed gray areas.

Again, the more a believer accepts that God has stated His will not just in generalities but also in specifics, the shorter is his list of personal liberties, and the greater becomes his sense of duty in Christian liberties. However, the less a saint of God acknowledges that God has specific steps for His children, not just a general path—"The steps of a good man are ordered by the LORD" (Ps. 37:23)—the longer becomes his list of supposed personal liberties, and the lesser grows his sense of responsibility with regard to Christian liberty.

Much of the reasoning for calling most gray areas by that name is the erroneous conclusion that since God has given no commandment on a particular subject, God has not spoken at all on that subject. Next, the conclusion gets carried a step farther when that person says that since God has not spoken on that particular subject, it is up to the individual to determine his own position. In determining of one's own position when God has made known the right position, the delicate balance between soul liberty and personal liberty is blurred. Furthermore, choosing of one's own "belief" when God has stated truth on a subject actually diminishes that issue from its place in God's will to a position where it "doesn't matter."

Also, while biblical Christianity is not about dictating belief or belief systems, it remains that believers will one day be judged at the Judgment Seat of Christ based upon what God believes, not based upon twenty-first century norms.

christian liberty
and the word of God

The most important fact about Christian liberty is that it is governed. The first governing agent for all appropriate expression of this liberty that believers possess is God's Word itself. The psalmist stated the concept that Scripture limits the expression of the believer's liberty when he wrote "And I will walk at liberty: for I seek thy precepts" (Ps. 119:45). The word "for" in Psalm 119:45 carries the meaning of the subordinating conjunction *because* in a cause-effect context. The overriding cause in the psalmist's life—and by extension the believer's life—is the seeking of God's precepts, the specifics of God's instruction (See Mark 10:5 and Hebrews 9:19 for confirmation that a precept is a specific instruction). The effect or consequence of this search of God's precepts is that the searcher ends up walking at liberty, that is, walking in true spiritual freedom. The psalmist clearly understood that Christian liberty is always subject to finding the truth of the Word of God; furthermore, he stated the fact that Christian liberty can never be attained outside the boundaries of obedience to God's Word.

All true freedom abides within defined boundaries. Every nation in the world has boundary lines with other nations on land, in air and sometimes in water. Every nation expects its neighboring nations to respect those boundaries. When those boundaries are mutually respected, there is peace between those nations. The legality of a person's residence in any given country is judged by his possession of citizenship rights within the agreed-upon boundary lines of his particular country.

Every property owner in every civilization that has ever existed on planet Earth has understood the need for boundaries. In fact, men invest small fortunes to determine exact locations of boundary lines for purposes of building, taxation and maintenance. Peace between adjacent property owners is maintained when both respect the agreed-upon property line.

Every game ever invented has boundary lines; balls or pucks or birdies are judged foul or fair, in-bounds or out-of-bounds, in-play or out-of-play, based upon the arbitrary placement of boundary lines. Liberty to continue playing the game is contingent upon the judgment of referees and umpires based upon the placement of lines.

God is not copying man in this matter. No. God created man in His own image and part of God's image for man in this world includes limits. Even in man's sinful state, he bows unwittingly to the image of his Creator in setting up boundaries in life. Why then should it be thought acceptable or reasonable that man would operate without boundaries in his faith? Why then should any person believe that he could have liberty without limits, belief without boundaries or persuasion without parameters? It simply cannot be.

> *"According as his divine power hath given unto us all things that pertain unto life and godliness, through the knowledge of him that hath called us to glory and virtue:*
>
> *"Whereby are given unto us exceeding great and precious promises: that by these ye might be partakers of the divine nature, having escaped the corruption that is in the world through lust."*—
> II Pet. 1:3, 4.

God obviously "left not himself without witness" (Acts 14:17) in Creation and in revelation. God has a word on every subject known to man and that word can be discovered. Indeed, that word must be discovered before any individual can walk in true Christian liberty.

God has indeed spoken, but not all His words are in commandments clearly stating, "Thou shalt" or "Thou shalt not." Some of God's speaking is in laws whereby He states eternal, unchangeable principles by which He deals with mankind specifically and Creation generally, as exemplified in His law of male and female. Still other examples of God's speaking are in His testimonies of individuals and groups of people down through history.

Again, God's speaking may be found in this statute, the statements in which He limits man's activities, as shown in God's limiting of marriage to one man and one woman. God's speaking may also come in the form of His judgments in which He states a certain thing or activity to be good or evil, as in the case of His saying that it is good for a man to draw near to God. To limit God's pleasure on any subject to commandments only is to deny much of what God has expressed that will ultimately please or displease Him.

Consider that our Lord never dictated a command, saying, "Ye shall worship both Sunday morning and Sunday evening." Instead, the Lord left a testimony that one can clearly see in a paralleling of the four Gospel records that it was on the first day of the week that the risen Christ met for communion and commission with His disciples and that He met with them both in the morning and in the evening of that first day.

Consider also that our Savior did not issue a command, saying, "Ye shall order thy calendar by seasons." No; but what did He do? He established a law of creative order that says, "While the earth remaineth, seedtime and harvest, and cold and heat, and summer and winter, and day and night shall not cease" (Gen. 8:22).

At the coming judgment believers "must all appear before the judgment seat of Christ; that every one may receive the things done in his body, according to that he hath done, whether it be good or bad" (II Cor. 5:10). Furthermore, "every one of us shall give account of himself to God" (Rom. 14:12). Note that is says every deed and every believer. Furthermore, it declares either good or bad, but not gray.

Good or bad. What kind of God would Jehovah be if He judged believers but had previously left them here with no direction as to whether a particular behavior was going to be judged favorably or unfavorably? God would be unjust to expect righteous behavior had He left us no means to determine right from wrong. However, God has left us an accurate record, a complete guide, a full-length book, an authoritative resource. From the Bible, one may know without doubt or question what he is supposed to do on any subject and in any situation pertinent to godliness.

Indeed, the long gray-area list is not a biblical list; rather, it is a disobedient believer's list, a compromiser's list and in our day more and more often becoming a five-point fundamentalist's list to justify decisions and activities that God does not approve or bless.

christian liberty and biblical charity

It was previously stated that the first governor for Christian liberty is Scripture. Truly, the Bible has governed all expression of Christian liberty. A close second to the Scripture in the governing or regulating of Christian liberty is biblical charity.

Charity as understood in modern times is only vaguely similar to what God meant by that word in Scripture. Modern dictionaries define the word *charity* in terms of benevolence, good will, generosity and even liberalness and leniency toward the needy, but with no mention of God or God's divine love is listed. One dictionary even cites mercy as a synonym for charity. Such failure to clarify the heights to which the wonderful biblical word *charity* attains is akin to describing Mt. Everest as a small hill on the borders of Nepal and of Tibet!

The stated definition of the biblical word *charity* is "the bond of perfectness" (Col. 3:14), an infinitely greater meaning than any stretch of benefaction or love of man to man! This word appears twenty-eight times in twenty-four verses and is used only in the New Testament. One occurrence of the adverb *charitably* appears in Romans 14:15. In all the texts where this word is used, it is a translation of the Greek word Agape or one of its forms. Above and beyond these instances, there are dozens of verses of Scripture where agape is translated *love* in its verb usage because the word *charity* has no verb form in the English language. There are also dozens of verses of the Bible where agape is translated *love* as a noun, and in all those instances, the context will show that it is God's love, a specific love, a high and holy love that ascends beyond the mere capability of man, a love that descends to depths in excess of the weak and beggarly reach of man's good will and a love that is distinct in its characteristics.

Charity, then, is not man's best stab at benevolence, nor is its full extent realized in alms for the poor. All charity in the biblical sense is God's love in action in a believer's life. While all charity in the biblical sense is love, not all love in the biblical sense is the equivalent of charity. The Holy Spirit's definition, "the bond of perfectness," shows much about this word.

In its literal application the bond (or band) is a ligament or joint tie, as referenced in Colossians 2:19. A bond (or band) in the figurative usage as appears in Colossians 3:14 refers to a uniting or controlling principle. The idea is the same whether literal or figurative. Both hold together. Both keep in control.

"Perfectness" as a specific word occurs nowhere else in the King James English Bible. This word means completeness as it applies to the growth of spiritual and moral character through Christ's Word by the controlling influence of Christ's indwelling Holy Spirit (Compare both Colossians 3:10–16 and Ephesians 4:23–5:20). This same root in other forms is translated "perfection" in Luke 8:14 and Hebrews 6:1 and 7:11. Its meaning in those other instances, although having a different noun ending, is the same as understood by the simple fact that the English suffixes -*ness* and -*ion* both make nouns and give the meaning of "the state or condition of." Therefore, both "perfectness" and "perfection" mean "the state or condition of being perfect (complete)."

Combined, then, biblical charity as defined by the Word of God is the uniting or controlling principle of the condition of spiritual and moral completeness. This uniting and controlling is nothing other than the filling of the Spirit of God. It is "the unity of the Spirit" (Eph. 4:3) and the control that the Spirit has when He fills (5:18) the believer. Biblical charity is, by extension and application, the fullness of the Person of Jesus Christ alive and working through the Holy Spirit in a child of the Heavenly Father.

Charity can be accurately said to be the character of Christ being lived out by the power of the Holy Spirit through the life of a child of God. The validity of these statements is made all the more secure with words from Paul's prayer:

> "*That ye, being rooted and grounded in love* (agape),
>
> "*May be able to comprehend with all saints what is the breadth,*

and length, and depth, and height;

"And to know the love (agape) *of Christ, which passeth knowledge, that ye might be filled with all the fulness of God."*— Eph. 3:17–19.

The listing of four dimensions when man is able to comprehend only three explains the phrase, "which passeth knowledge." What glorious and divine love this is! In truth, this charity, this love, is Christ living in the believer; furthermore, knowing that love and being filled with His fullness involves a supernatural dimension, a dimension which can be none other than the Holy Spirit's infinite infilling, influencing, informing and infusing. Indeed, the only way the Bible recognizes that "the love (agape) of God is shed abroad in our hearts [is] by the Holy Ghost which is given unto us" (Rom. 5:5).

christian liberty and offense

The third governor or regulator of Christian liberty involves offense. In the study of Christian liberty, one encounters *offense* and *offend*, the noun and verb form of the same word. Today, offense is almost always linked to the hurting of one's feelings, a connection that is never in play in the Bible. Proof that biblical offense is not the hurting of a person's feelings is found in Psalm 119:165, which says, "Great peace have they which love thy law: and nothing shall offend them."

Indeed, if offense were the hurting of a person's feelings, then no one could ever lay claim to loving the Bible, because no person has ever lived long without having his feelings hurt. Even the best believers endure hurt feelings almost every day of their lives. This verse in its immediate context appears in the Psalm devoted to the praise and exaltation of the revelation of God. Correctly understood, it states that no person who loves the Word of God will ever be offended (in the biblical sense) by anything in the Word of God.

What, then, is offense in Scripture? It is, at times, sin or iniquity itself. In other instances, it is any action on the part of one person that leads or influences another person, of whatever spiritual station, into sin or iniquity. In approximately eighty references in God's Book, not one Hebrew or Greek word translated *offend* ever indicates the hurting of a person's feelings.

Quite honestly, hurt feelings in the record of the Bible are dealt with in a manner starkly foreign to the spoiled, feelings-exalting culture of our day. The manner of dealing with hurt feelings according to the Bible should never be confused with or combined with God's teachings concerning that which is sin and that which influences or eases the way for someone else to sin.

To be accurate, the Hebrew and Greek words behind the English word *offense* have meanings such as "covert action," "guilt," "perversion," "crime," "penalty," "sin," "stumbling block," "enticement," "obstacle," "trespass," "apostasy," "quarrel," "injustice," "error," "transgression," "occasion of stumbling," "failure," "entrapment" and "snare." In all Christian liberty, then, there must be the governing principle that no liberty ever entertained, if said liberty might be the cause for an observer to stumble or be weakened.

The entire explanation is necessary for accuracy in one's apprehension of Christian liberty. The undeniable relation that exists between true liberty and the subjects of charity and offenses brings a serious-minded believer to the right position, a position that acknowledges that true Christian liberty is recognizable as freedom only to a spiritual person with a spiritual mind.

The carnal mind, at enmity with God, will ever seek to

express liberty in carnal ways. What the spiritual mind realizes, paradoxically, is that true Christian liberty actually requires self-imposed restriction for the benefit of others! In other words, spiritual people practice that now-antiquated concept known as *death to self* when practicing their Christian liberty.

Although carnal reasoning will be loath to admit this, the life with the most liberty is the strictest Christian life, not the loosest one!

christian liberty in I corinthians

Chapters eight through ten of first Corinthians is part of the letter written to a church with many carnality-oriented problems. In this portion the apostle Paul discussed the Christian liberty of first-century believers to eat meat offered to idols. Notice that at the very outset in the first verse, Paul coordinates this teaching on liberty with the edifying quality of charity: "Knowledge puffeth up, but charity edifieth." Notice that two verses later, he wrote, "If any man love (Agape) God, the same is known of him."

Charity, in this case extended to mean a biblical love for God from the heart of a believer, will never puff up a believer practicing his liberty; it will always edify those who observe the one practicing the liberty. Charity is never in play when one believer is attempting to take advantage of another believer, when one believer is using his knowledge and ability to overshadow another believer, or when one believer is neglecting to show deference or forbearance toward another believer. Charity is not in the driver's seat when a saint of God is demanding that he has this or that right, or when a child of God is argumentatively and defiantly living out what he thinks is his liberty. The controlling influence of God's love flowing through a believer in Holy Spirit power will always edify, build, strengthen and empower other believers to do right.

Later in I Corinthians the Spirit of God lists fifteen separate ways that charity is demonstrated in the life of a believer who allows God's love to be the controlling influence in his life. This list makes it abundantly clear that this charity is not the result of a good person turning better, but rather the outworking of the in-worked Christ by the power of the Holy Ghost. No mere erotic or brotherly love could affect such a demonstration.

> *"Charity suffereth long, and is kind; charity envieth not; charity vaunteth not itself, is not puffed up,*

> *"Doth not behave itself unseemly, seeketh not her own, is not easily provoked, thinketh no evil;*

> *"Rejoiceth not in iniquity, but rejoiceth in the truth;*

> *"Beareth all things, believeth all things, hopeth all things, endureth all things.*

> *"Charity never faileth."*—I Cor. 13:4–8.

When God's love is the controlling force in a Spirit-filled believer, he will exhibit longsuffering, not abruptness; kindness, not cruelty; meekness, not envy; quietness, not boastfulness; humility, not pride; appropriateness, not debauchery; selflessness, not selfishness; patience, not agitation; trust, not suspicion, joy in truth, not in sin; forbearance, not rejection; belief, not doubt; hope, not despair; endurance, not fainting; and success, not failure.

This list absolutely destroys the gray-area justification for many distracting compromises not only being allowed but also being promoted among Christians, including independent Baptists in this millennium.

Once again, returning to the eighth chapter of I Corinthians, Paul moved from relating charity to the proper expression of

Christian liberty to relating offense to a correct expression of Christian liberty. The concept that a believer could eat meat offered to idols was clear. The idol meant nothing. It was a dead god: a stone, a stick. It could not see, hear, feel, act, taste or smell. It was blind, deaf, dumb, numb and paralyzed. What then, did the Spirit of God through Paul say next? He warned the believers who knew the truth about idols and who could rightly enter into that liberty and enjoy it to "take heed lest by any means this liberty of yours become a stumblingblock to them that are weak" (vs. 9). Paul continued in the next verse by citing a probable hypothetical situation: the scenario of a person with a weak conscience observing the believer in Jesus Christ eating meat offered to an idol and thus being made bolder in his unsaved or unsanctified beliefs.

What was the Spirit's conclusion, then, concerning believers who had both knowledge and liberty with regard to the people who had neither? First, God said that enjoying that liberty in the presence of a lost idolator could result in that lost man continuing in his idolatry and ultimately going to Hell (vs. 11). Second, he said that enjoying that liberty in the presence of a weak brother was a sin against Christ (vs. 12). Third, and finally, the Holy Spirit said that the spiritual position was abstinence from the liberty altogether: "If meat make my brother to offend, I will eat no flesh while the world standeth, lest I make my brother to offend" (vs. 13). It becomes clearer and clearer as one reads the Bible that the Christian life lived in Christian liberty is not the loose "I-can-do-anything-because-God-doesn't-stop-me" life. What grows in undeniable evidence is that the Christian life lived in Christian liberty is a life of strict adherence to the highest of spiritual, moral and ethical standards.

Paul's discussion, that one restrain not the Holy Spirit's revelation regarding Liberty, continues in the ninth chapter of

I Corinthians. In that chapter, the writer employed the word *power* five times (vss. 4–6, 12, 18). What is this word? It is the identical Greek word translated *liberty* in chapter eight! It means "privilege," "freedom" and even "authority." It covers the concept of "a right or an inherent, delegated allowance due to one's position."

While the English word is different, its meaning is not. The subject is still Christian liberty, that is, what believers have the privilege and freedom and authority to do, what God has delegated to His children because of their position in His sight.

The narrative of chapter nine deals with Paul's apostleship, his ministry in the Gospel, and his freedom (note use of word *free* in vss. 1, 19). What Paul was doing in this chapter was demonstrating to the carnal, worldly Corinthians that he was not commanding them to live strictly while he lived loosely. He was delineating the ways in which he was living the way he had just told them to live in the previous chapter. After teaching the carnal Corinthians to forsake the carnality of demanding their rights and to live in true charity and liberty without offending others, Paul concluded, "But I have used none of these things: neither have I written these things that it should be so done unto me…". Paul was not living a loose, rights-demanding, liberty-flaunting life. He was living the strictest of strict lives.

Chapter nine continues with a passage that has been misused to justify nearly every compromise of twenty-first-century so-called Christianity. Instead of this passage teaching that believers have liberty to do whatever they please, this portion strongly supports the context that the life of true Christian liberty is the careful life, not the careless one; the life with standards and structure, not the life without them. Paul stated that he was indeed free, at liberty, that is, from all men (vs. 19). What did that freedom prompt him to do? Did he use that freedom to enjoy himself? No, a thousand times, no. He recognized that freedom, that liberty, that privilege, that right; and then he set aside all that Christian liberty and 'made [him]self servant unto all, that [he] might gain the more' (vs. 19). Paul followed the strictest of Jewish requirements when he was attempting to reach Jews so he would not offend them. Paul adhered to the strictest of law-keeping when he was among law-keepers, so that he would not offend them. Paul abided by the strictest of social expectations when he was ministering to those without law to avoid offending them. Paul held to the strictest of the codes of decency and honor when working among the weak so he would not offend them. Paul did *not* say, "I am made all things to all men, that I might by *some* means save all."

He said, "I am made all things to all men, that I might by *all* means save some" (vs. 22).

Finally, in I Corinthians, chapter 9, Paul concluded with an athletic illustration using rules of athletic games. The temperate man striving for the mastery so that he may win the crown is not the athlete who takes all the liberty he can; rather, he is the competitor who lives the strictest life and follows the strictest regimen so that he may be the best prepared. Again, Scripture utilizes the plainest of terms to prove that lives lived in true Christian liberty are not careless and lawless but are observant to temperance and qualification and requirement and discipline.

While chapter 10 moves into some other subjects, strains of the liberty discussion remain. Notably, Paul wrote of "the cup of blessing which we bless" and "the bread which we break" (vs. 16) in stark contrast to "that which is offered in sacrifice to idols" (vs. 19). Again, the meats issue arose (vss. 25–28) so that the Holy Ghost could drive home once again the fact that just because a believer possesses a liberty, there are times when he would be carnal to practice that liberty, when he would not act in biblical charity if he practiced that liberty and when he would offend others if he practiced that liberty.

Indeed, the liberty existed because of the twice-repeated statement "all things are lawful for me" (vs. 23). Obviously, the "all things" of that verse meant all things that were liberties. Paul did not mean all things including sins and iniquities; idolatry and dishonor of parents and theft and adultery and lying and covetousness were not lawful for anyone. He was keeping the context and referencing issues of liberty. What, then, was the Spirit's rebuttal to all liberty issues being lawful? The Spirit of God stated that they might be lawful but neither expedient nor edifying, and the concept of edification reverts to the very opening verse of this entire Spirit-inspired, Spirit-preserved discussion: "Charity edifieth" (8:1).

Once again, the Christian life that is lived in the spiritual way of Christian liberty is classified as the strict life:

"Let no man seek his own, but every man another's wealth."

"Whether therefore ye eat, or drink, or whatsoever ye do, do all to the glory of God.

"Give none offence, neither to the Jews, nor to the Gentiles, nor to the church of God:

"Even as I please all men in all things, not seeking mine own profit, but the profit of many, that they may be saved."—10:24, 31–33.

One must realize that each Book of the Bible is its own context within the larger context of all Scripture. Therefore, the "all things" of verse thirty-three again is all liberty issues including even the simplest of life functions such as eating and drinking. Paul was not declaring that he could become a man-pleaser; indeed, were Paul or any other believer to become a man-pleaser before becoming a God-pleaser, he would not be seeking the profit of others for them to be saved nor would he "be the servant of Christ" (Gal. 1:10).

The revelatory method of the Spirit of God usually mentions a topic in an introductory statement and then gives details of that topic. When the Spirit of God moves on to other topics, however, He often references the previously-discussed topic. So it is that in I Corinthians 11:27–29 in the discussion of the eating of the Lord's Supper, believers are cautioned about partaking unworthily. While it may not be absolutely provable, it is absolutely probable that at least one way that a believer partakes of the Lord's table unworthily and fails to discern the Lord's body is to partake with a heart that insists on rights and liberties and never defers to the lost or to the weaker believers.

christian liberty in romans

Romans, chapter 14, is a chapter that mentions the eating of meats as well as the observance of days. The word *liberty* is not found in that portion, but the word *charitably* is (vs. 15). Obviously, if the eating of meats offered to idols was a Christian liberty issue in idolatrous Corinth, it was just as much a Christian liberty issue in pagan Rome. Just so, the observance of certain holy days—holidays—was a Christian liberty issue in the capital city of the empire. Many such holy days were days set aside for the respect and worship of the members of the Roman and Greek pantheons, not to exclude the emperor worship of the day.

One item that must be clear is that this passage does not teach that believers have liberty to neglect or desecrate the Lord's Day. God's teaching about the first day of the week is not a liberty issue. God has spoken in concrete terms and constraining tones with regard to the church's responsibility to recognize and respect the first day of each week as a day of worship, rest and spiritual pursuit. Contextually and grammatically, the mention of meats offered to idols, a liberty issue, makes the day-observance issue also a liberty. Transcended to modern times, this would correspond to a believer's liberty to observe national, religious or even personal commemorative holidays.

Therefore, although the word *liberty* is not found in Romans 14, the chapter does address Christian liberties. Once again, it is abundantly clear that the Christian life with true liberty is the strict Christian life, not the loose one. Two verses seem to summarize the whole chapter:

> *"For he that in these things serveth Christ is acceptable to God, and approved of men.*
>
> *"Let us therefore follow after the things which make for peace, and things wherewith one may edify another."*—Vss. 18, 19.

Clearly, if a Spirit-filled believer must choose between being acceptable to God or being approved of men, he must choose the former; however, when it is possible to do both, the Spirit-filled believer will do both. He will not smugly hide behind his being acceptable to God in some matter of liberty while he justifies offending others and failing to edify them. Why not? Because such justification results in unnecessary disapproval of men.

In verse three, Paul wrote that people who exercise a liberty should not despise those who do not and that those who do not exercise a liberty should not criticize those who do. The entire premise of despising (holding in light esteem or disrespect) and criticizing is mutually exclusive of biblical charity. One cannot possess charity at the same moment he is despising a brother who denies himself a liberty. Neither can one possess charity while he is castigating one who engages in that same liberty. In the case of eating, both gave God thanks for what they ate (vs. 6). In the instance of holidays, both regarded the day as a day the Lord had made (vs. 7). Because no man lives or dies to himself, but all men live and die to the Lord, each believer should keep his eyes upon the Judgment Seat of Christ (vss. 8–12) when Christ's perfect judgment "will bring to light the hidden things of darkness, and will make manifest the counsels of the hearts" (I Cor. 4:5).

Another great truth of Romans 14 is that being both acceptable to God and approved of men prohibits casting stumbling blocks into one's pathway or offenses into his environment. The believer is not to judge the other man's motives but to judge his own motions. Notice I Thessalonians 5:21, 22:

> *"Prove all things; hold fast that which is good.*
>
> *"Abstain from all appearance of evil."*

The spiritual believer, fully aware of and subjected to this biblical injunction, will go through the garden of his life and pull out every weed of anything that could cause stumbling, every stray growth that could lead to others' offense and every wild gourd that would contribute toward others' weaknesses.

Continuing through Romans 14, the Spirit points out that enjoying a liberty to the grief of another is not charitable (vs. 15). Any issue that is a liberty issue is neither clean nor unclean (vs. 14) but pure (vs. 20). However, the pursuit of that liberty and the decision whether or not to enjoy it are what must be considered.

Interestingly, verse sixteen does not say, "Let not then your sin be evil spoken of." Evil should always be evil spoken of! The verse warns against forcing a good liberty upon someone else, causing him to speak evil of the good. The kingdom of God is far higher than physical meats and drinks; it is the spiritual qualities of "righteousness and peace and joy in the Holy Ghost" (vs. 17). Toward the end of Romans, chapter 14, one sees that enjoying a liberty to the grief of another is not good. Again, the liberty issue itself is not wrong, but the attitude about it can be. The work of God involves the lost souls of them "for whom Christ died" (vs. 15) as well as the souls of them who are already brothers in Christ. The summary for this section is this: "It is good neither to eat flesh, nor to drink wine, nor any thing whereby thy brother stumbleth, or is offended, or is made weak" (vs. 21). This verse does not say, "Whereby thy brother may stumble, be offended, or be made weak." The use of the word "is" as the auxiliary to all three verbs makes the eating of certain foods, the drinking of certain drinks, and the engaging in certain activities—Christian liberties, if you please—the potential cause for others to stumble, to take offense and to be weakened.

The closing verses of chapter fourteen and the opening statements of chapter fifteen finalize this concept as to its treatment in Romans. Paul asked, "Hast thou faith? have it to thyself before God" (vs. 22). Lest this verse be used as it has been by some, to justify keeping one's faith to oneself and not witnessing and testifying of Christ, one must see that this is again referencing issues of liberty, not issues like the Gospel or the great truths of Scripture. In this statement, the Lord is teaching that regardless of the belief of the person with regard to his liberty, it is better to keep it quiet rather than to offend and fail to exhibit charity.

The person who demands of himself to put charity above his own freedom is "happy" because "he condemneth not himself in that thing which he alloweth." The person who requires of himself that he not offend others is "happy" because "he condemneth not himself in that thing which he alloweth" (vs. 22). What is this condemnation? It is the condemnation of failing to edify others through charity, the condemnation of offending others and causing them to have occasion to sin.

Any doubt about the matter of whether to engage in one's liberty or deny oneself the freedom of engaging in it are settled in the last verse of the chapter, which says, "Whatsoever is not of faith is sin." Again, in a verse that is often misapplied, the idea is that if a person cannot have absolute assurance and peace from God—faith, that is—that he can enjoy his liberty in charity and without offense, he would be in sin to enjoy that liberty. This is in absolute agreement with I Corinthians 8:12 that states that wounding the weak conscience of another is a sin against Christ.

In conclusion to this grand concept, Paul wrote under Holy Spirit's inspiration,

> *"We then that are strong ought to bear the infirmities of the weak, and not to please ourselves.*
>
> *"Let every one of us please his neighbor for his good to edification.*
>
> *"For even Christ pleased not himself; but, as it is written, The reproaches of them that reproached thee fell on me."*—15:1–3.

How beautifully God's Spirit tied together the obvious fact that, indeed, the Christian life lived in Christian liberty is the self-restricted, self-mortified life, the life of death to self. Christian liberty, then, is not about pleasing self but about pleasing others to their edification. Christian liberty, then, is not about self-expression of one's corrupt passions, carnal preferences, or compromising privilege, but about enduring the reproaches of Christ.

christian liberty in galatians

Galatians, chapter 5, is yet another portion pertinent to this topic. The unspiritual position of entering into and enjoying liberties regardless of the impact of such living upon others completely ignores the Spirit's instruction in Galatians 5:13: "For brethren, ye have been called unto liberty; only use not liberty for an occasion to the flesh, but by love serve one another." The love here is agape.

The specific liberty of the believers in the fifth chapter of Galatians concerned their New Testament freedom to bypass the circumcision of their male children. Paul rejected that Jewish tradition when he said, "For in Jesus Christ neither circumcision availeth any thing, nor uncircumcision; but faith with worketh by love" (vs. 6). Again, the love is Agape.

Paul continued by saying that he yearned for those Judaizers who were requiring circumcision for salvation and for sanctification to be cut off, because they were troubling not only sinners who needed to comprehend saving grace but also vulnerable new believers who needed to apprehend living grace.

However, the response of the New Testament Gentile believers, in biblical charity and liberty, was not to say, "Hey, you Judaizers, we have liberty. You can take your circumcision and go fly a kite. We don't have to do that anymore. Na-na-na-na-na!" That would have been the biting and devouring of one another referenced in Galatians 5:15. The charity-liberty-no-offense response was for the New Testament Gentile believers to serve the Jewish believers and not use their release from circumcision as an occasion to the flesh. The proper response, to avoid offense, was for those New Testament Gentile believers to submit to circumcision. "For all the law is fulfilled in one word, even in this;

Thou shalt love thy neighbour as thyself" (vs. 14).

christian liberty in james

The Lord's half-brother, James, pastor of the Jerusalem church and moderator of the Jerusalem council (Acts 15), gave to the church yet another definitive and authoritative aspect of Christian liberty.

The apostle spoke of the law of liberty on two occasions (1:25; 2:12). This phrase would be ridiculous if Christian liberty were the lawless abandon that seems to be the agenda of some compromising fundamentalists of today. However, the law of liberty is not ridiculous; it is most sensible. It is the governing principle by which God operates in the affairs of men with regard to their liberties.

The context of James 1:22–2:26 donates much wisdom, then, to the topic of Christian liberty. Contextually, the Word (1:22) and the law of liberty (1:25) and the royal law (2:8) are equivalent and synonymous. The idea is that God's revelation in Scripture gives God's guidelines for the expressions of and the experiences of liberty. The entire foundation upon which this portion is based is the opening statement: "But be ye doers of the word, and not hearers only, deceiving your own selves" (1:22). In other words, the person who misuses his Christian liberties is a self-deceived soul who resembles a person who gets up in the morning, stares at his disheveled hair, unbrushed teeth and wrinkled pajamas and does nothing about it, regardless of how unpleasant he may look to others. This illustration parallels all that has already been said about the misuse of Christian liberty.

He who misuses his Christian liberties cares little how he appears to others. Even after having understood from "the word" what he is responsible to do, he "goeth his way, and straightway forgetteth what manner of man he was" (vs. 24).

By contrast, the person who properly uses his Christian liberties, "looketh into the perfect law of liberty, and continueth therein, he being not a forgetful hearer, but a doer of the work, this man shall be blessed in his deed" (vs. 25). What is this work in which such a man is blessed? What is this deed that he does? It is obvious from context that the blessed deed is any deed performed in obedience to principles of the law of liberty.

First, note in James 1:26 and 27 that all such deeds in which this man is blessed are works that separate from popularity. Professedly fundamentalist Christians "seem to be" religious (spiritual) when they are not; furthermore, they seem not to be worldly, but they are spotted by the world. The spots may be few or many, but spots are spots. A shirt with four grease spatters down the front is 99% clean, but the spots make the wearer toss it into the dirty laundry and change shirts. So, then, five-point fundamentalists should clean up their spots, however many or few.

Next, the blessed deed is a deed that avoids partiality. James 2:1–11 is the Scripture classic on what the Lord called respect of persons, what has become known in our vernacular as favoritism or partiality. The particular example that James cites is noticing a rich man and neglecting a poor man. James denounced this noticing-neglecting pattern as being partial, as being evidence of evil thought-judgment and as being respectful of the very people who damaged the cause of Christ. While independent Baptists who are engaging in compromise do not so much practice the rich versus poor aspect of noticing and neglecting, their brand of noticing and neglecting is in the arena of convenient versus inconvenient. Being extra careful not to go as far to the left as the Neo-Evangelicals, they nonetheless go left in the general direction of compromise toward convenience in selecting their mentors, methods, music and so on. Somewhat like the centurion in Acts 27:11, they follow the reasoning of "the master and the owner of the ship, more than those things…spoken" by the Lord, the apostles and the prophets.

Careful scrutiny of James' treatise in this chapter shows that this behavior is a violation of loving one's neighbor as oneself and a violation of the second greatest of all Jesus' commandments. Not surprisingly, the love mentioned in James 2:5 and 8 is agape, the same word translated *charity,* the same word depicting the fullness of the character of Christ in the believer.

Furthermore, this agape love is the same quality that would prevent such noticing-neglecting and lead the believer into walking charitably.

Finally, the blessed deed in this portion is a deed that shuns hypocrisy. James 2:12–26 is divided into three sections, each ending with the declaration that faith without works is dead (vss. 17, 20, 26). Each of the separate passages (James 2:12-17, 18–20, 21–26) identifies a definite way that the misuse of Christian liberty is rank hypocrisy. It goes without mention that James is not referring to the faith by which a sinner is saved from sin. The portion has nothing to do with the deliverance of lost souls from the eternal flames of condemnation. When the apostle asked in verse 14, "Can faith save him?" he was not asking if faith alone saves a man from going to Hell.

Conversely, the question as to whether faith can save is asked in light of whether or not faith that has no accompanying works can save a man from the judgment of the law of liberty that is mentioned just two verses prior! This judgment, that of the "perfect law of liberty," is a judgment that James said would be "without mercy" upon those who had "shewed no mercy"; moreover, James added that "mercy rejoiceth against judgment" (vs. 13). What is this about? It is the Holy Spirit's setting of the foundation for everything else written in the second chapter of James. In short, the person who lives charitably as Scripture unfolds the definition of charity, loving his neighbor as himself, will show mercy to those around him by not abrasively demanding his rights but by lovingly denying his rights. The works that prove faith, in this context, are not works to earn salvation but works that prove salvation. Nothing proves salvation more than a person denying himself a clearly-given liberty. Therefore, works that are motivated by an honest understanding of Christian liberty, as Scripture teaches liberty, will be the kind of works that produce rejoicing when the law of liberty is the plumb line and the standard of judgment. These works are works carried out with the full recognition of the existence of weaker, more vulnerable souls who would be offended easily by advantage-seeking, rights-demanding believers, the very people James said had dead faith.

First, note that the hypocritical believer who misuses his liberty and despises his opportunities to live in light of biblical charity has an unprofitable faith. Twice, James says of such a selfish faith, "What doth it profit?" (2:14, 16). The understood antecedent of "it" in that four-word question is professed faith that does not display itself via works that are performed in full light of the right understanding of Christian liberty. Profit, as presented by James, has nothing to do with money; instead, the word refers to a resulting advantage or an ensuing benefit.

In other words, James rhetorically asked, "What possible benefit does a person bestow upon others when his faith does not prompt him to engage in loving works that give people what they really need?" Again, though James cites food, clothing and things "needful to the body," his application is far deeper. In essence, he is stating that an individual who would not get a coat out of his closet or a loaf of bread from his cupboard for a man with temporal needs would certainly never step outside the comfort zone of his rights to supply for the spiritual needs of another.

Secondly, James points out that the hypocritical believer who misuses his liberty and refuses to take opportunity to live out biblical charity possesses an unproven faith. It is a faith that dares to believe that life without the proof of works that display a scriptural understanding of charity and liberty is the sum total of Christian living. This faith has never been tested in light of James 1:1–12 and as a result is still infantile and shallow. It is a faith that arises in conversation but never ascends in consecration. It is a faith that has not yet considered that all claims must have visible and viable evidence if those claims are to be accepted as realistic. It is a faith no more helpful to those around that individual than the faith of "devils [who] also believe" that "there is one God" is to those devils.

In the third place, the apostle James declares that a hypocritical believer who misuses liberty and shuns his opportunities to demonstrate biblical charity is a believer living with unperfected faith. The two personages of Old Testament history, Abraham and Rahab, do not at first seem to present any parallels. One was a patriarch of the faith and the other, a harlot. What common ground did these two share? Interestingly, these two mentioned together in six verses of context are also cited together in Hebrews 11:17 and 31. Both these passages mention the same two things: Abraham's offering of Isaac and Rahab's protection of the Hebrew spies. A thorough exegesis of these two events is not necessary. Simply put, Abraham's faith was perfected by his willingness to offer up Isaac and his belief that God would raise Isaac from the dead if indeed Isaac were to die. Just as simply put, Rahab's faith was perfected by her willingness to endanger her own life to spare the people of God. (Incidentally, Rahab's lie is not mentioned in Hebrews or James and is never praised; it is her faith that is mentioned and praised.)

When a believer denies his rights and lives his life in light of the needs of others and in light of the influence he has on others and in light of possible high cost to himself, his faith is perfected. Perfected faith graduates a person from the moment when his faith is counted for righteousness to the moment when he proves he is a friend of God as opposed to a friend of the world (Jas. 4:4, 5). Perfected faith graduates a person from the moment when the terror of the Lord has dawned upon one's soul to the point of salvation (Josh. 2:9–11) to the moment when he proves he will protect God's people from harm before he protects himself. Incidentally the two events of faith in Abraham's life were separated by slightly over half a century; the two events of faith in Rahab's life were separated by about forty years. Faith is not perfected overnight, but true faith will be perfected nevertheless!

christian liberty illustrated

An example from the life of Timothy aptly illustrates the willingness of a believer to bypass a liberty in order to avoid causing others to stumble, take offense or become weakened. Timothy was the son of a Greek who had married a Jewess. Timothy's mother Eunice and her mother Lois had come to faith in Christ. Through their testimony (II Tim. 1:5) Timothy had also trusted Christ. By the time that Paul met this unique young man, he had grown in grace to the point that he was "well reported of by the brethren that were at Lystra and Iconium" (Acts 16:2). As Paul observed Timothy, he began to sense not only Timothy's spirituality but also the Holy Spirit's direction to select Timothy as his serving-traveling companion to replace John Mark, who had only recently accompanied his uncle Barnabas to Cyprus.

Just prior to his arrival at Lystra and Iconium, Paul had attended and participated in the Jerusalem council. The Spirit of God saw fit to cover the Jerusalem council (the only multi-church council cited in Scripture) in the Book of Acts. Therefore, it behooves modern-day believers to examine the issues of that council, specifically the issues of law and works versus grace and faith.

Oversimplified, the Jerusalem council was the point of decision in which it was understood that the ceremonial law provisions of the Old Testament Aaronic priesthood no longer applied to the New Testament worship and approach to God. Indeed, this was the gathering of spiritual leaders that publicly recognized that "the priesthood being changed, there is made of necessity a change also of the law" (Heb. 7:12).

Again oversimplified, that same Jerusalem council arrived at a strong statement that the New Testament church was required to maintain God's eternal law. James, the pastor of the Jerusalem church and moderator of the council, handed down the sentence that New Testament churches and their individual members, "abstain from pollutions of idols, and from fornication, and from things strangled, and from blood" (Acts 15:20, concepts repeated in Acts 15:29; 21:25).

While abandoning those aspects of the ancient Levitical order that were entirely Jewish, this congregation of apostles and church fathers taught the absolute need not to abandon any law, commandment, statute or judgment that remained as part of God's eternal law. The eternal law of God addresses New Testament requirements, not options. The use of the word "abstain" shows that. This abstinence was obviously volitional. Just as no one forces another to commit sin, neither does anyone force another to commit righteousness. The statement in Acts 15:29 that "if ye keep yourselves from these, ye shall do well" has an obvious opposite that if one does not keep himself from these, he does not do well.

This abstinence was in four specific areas. First, New Testament churches in general and their members individually were to engage in a spiritual abstinence. The phrase, "pollutions of idols," refers to idolatry itself along with all the defiling spiritual damage originating with or accompanying sacrifices and offerings to false gods. This phrase includes the soiling and dirtying of spirit, soul and life that is associated with any aspect of worship of or service to any false god. The repetition of this principle in Acts 15:29 makes clear the fact that this spiritual abstinence included "meats offered to idols," the same charity-liberty-offense issue cited previously in this chapter.

Second, New Testament churches corporately and their members individually were to practice moral abstinence from fornication. This word is used thirty-six times in Scripture to depict unfaithfulness to God via idolatry or unfaithfulness to one's fellow man via moral indecency. Fornication in the latter meaning includes a wide array of moral improprieties, a list of unsavory practices that due to a corrupting world culture gets longer with each passing generation. Adultery, incest, sodomy, lesbianism, homosexuality, pornography, bestiality and polygamy—these gross moral defilements and more were to be completely avoided by any person claiming to be Christ's. The basic reason for the council's requiring the abstinence from these heinous aberrations of God's eternal moral law was that any engagement in such sins would taint and possibly ruin beyond repair any individual, marriage, family, church, culture, people group or nation that would tolerate them.

In the third place, the Jerusalem council required New Testament churches as assemblies and the particular saints of their memberships to practice social abstinence. Specifically, the Gentile believers were required to abstain from choking animals to death as opposed to slitting their throats and draining the blood from them. This requirement was no more exclusive of other socially-offensive actions than was fornication exclusive of other morally-offensive actions. Rather, the strangling issue exemplified those cultural actions that could serve as stumbling blocks within the churches that were quickly becoming multicultural. In other words, the council invoked upon churches the need to identify any practice that could potentially result in spiritual offense to the populace and refrain from it.

Again, this was not to apply to doctrines and truths of Scripture, but to the social lifestyles of believers. By extension, this aspect of the abstinence policy easily shows one of many reasons it is unwise, indeed wrong, for believers to smoke, consume alcohol, use illicit drugs and so forth.

Fourth and finally, the godly men who met at Jerusalem in Acts 15 sentenced local churches and their members to a natural abstinence. The word *blood* found by itself in all three listings (15:20, 29; 21:25) is the word used elsewhere in Scripture to designate bloodshed, blood-guiltiness and violence. What is meant by this stipulation is that, while the New Testament church was to be the spiritual, moral and social compass for its community, it was never to become the legal avenger. The church was not to shed blood in forcing people to become believers. Evangelism was to be aggressive but not forceful. Discipleship was to be aggressive but not forceful. This clearly explains why Paul did not go from compelling believers to recant and blaspheme or face death to compelling unbelievers to believe and worship or face death. Even though other groups such as the Pharisees and Sadducees were guilty of killing and torturing noncompliant people, Christ's followers were never to resort to blood and threats to gain or keep converts.

Returning then to the towns of Lystra and Iconium and to Paul's encounter with Timothy, it is significant to note that the Jerusalem council had recently determined that believers did not have to be circumcised to be saved. The apostles—Paul among them—and elders who had decided that the Gentile believers had to engage in the four previously-cited abstinences had also concluded that circumcision was a strictly Jewish observance which was not necessary for Gentile believers. However, when Paul made the decision to have Timothy accompany him on his second missionary journey, he "took and circumcised him because of the Jews were in those quarters: for they knew all that his father was a Greek" (16:3).

Unquestionably, Timothy had Christian liberty to forego this painful—and at his age, humiliating—procedure. The council had just decided that this Jewish tradition was not to be taught as a necessity any more. James, the pastor at the Jerusalem church, said that the apostles should not "trouble...them, which from among the Gentiles are turned to God" (15:19). Why, then, did Paul take him and have him circumcised? Why did Timothy, who was certainly of age and of sound mind, submit? The answer is simple. Both of them understood that no Christian liberty can be practiced in charity if others are caused to stumble or to take offense or to become weak.

An interesting aside is that as soon as Timothy was healed from his surgery, he and Paul departed from Lystra and Iconium and Derbe to distribute to the churches "the decrees for to keep, that were ordained of the apostles and elders which were at Jerusalem. And so were the churches established in the faith, and increased in number daily" (16:4, 5). Timothy, still fresh from submission to circumcision, was helping to broadcast the decrees telling Gentile believers they did not have to submit to circumcision. He could have become upset that others were privileged to enjoy a liberty he could not enjoy; instead, he responded in Christian charity and bore the circumcision for the greater cause of Christ. Timothy lived a stricter life, not a looser life, in order to assist Paul in evangelizing sinners and edifying saints.

Because charity is God's love through the Holy Spirit in control of the believer and because biblical Christian liberty is always submitted to the truths and teachings of Scripture, a spiritually mature, Holy-Spirit-filled Christian is the only person who can fully understand what Paul wrote when he said,

> *"Now the Lord is that Spirit: and where the Spirit of the Lord is, there is liberty.*
>
> *"But we all, with open face beholding as in a glass the glory of the Lord, are changed into the same image from glory to glory, even as by the Spirit of the Lord."*—II Cor. 3:17, 18.

The beautiful meaning of this quotation is lost on people who want to justify carnal self-gratification and worldly pleasure by flippantly quoting, "Where the Spirit of the Lord is, there is liberty" to the exclusion of the contextual content! Paul wrote perhaps the most profound principle of all regarding biblical Christian liberty in this portion, inseparably linking all expression of that liberty to the Holy Spirit's work in the life a saint who is peering into the mirror of God's Word to behold God's glory so that he can be changed into that image. Such a devoted and consecrated child of God knows he is "predestinate[d] to be conformed to the image of his Son" (Rom. 8:29), and that such conformity is totally predicated upon his submitting to the Holy Spirit, his loving God, and his being called in accord with God's purpose (vs. 28).

Because of the commonplace misrepresentations of biblical charity and biblical Christian liberty in the religious climate of the United States of America in our generation, most churchgoers and religious people have no idea what offense-avoiding biblical charity and liberty are. The average American does not know what either one is, has never seen either one in practice, and has no capacity to wrap his brain around what either one of them is or looks like. Part of the fault for this cluelessness as to what charity and liberty are lies squarely upon the shoulders of leaders who still call themselves fundamentalists but have abandoned some of the true scriptural definition and application of these vital scriptural words in favor of the relevance movement!

Our churchgoing public is rather like a city boy who has never been out of the concrete jungle but is asked to comment on the behavior of a bull in a pasture. The child does not know what a bull is, has never seen a bull, and therefore, cannot form even a conceptual image of a bull. Furthermore, he does not know what a pasture is, has never seen a pasture, and therefore, cannot form in his mind a mental picture of a pasture. He will be utterly unable to describe a bull patrolling his pasture, occasionally snorting and pawing, sometimes aloofly surveying, generally grazing and resting, and occasionally charging perceived intruders.

Unless and until independent Baptists return to biblical boundaries, that city boy's understanding of the bull in the pasture will be our society's understanding of biblical Christianity. "What is written in the law? How readest thou?"

chapter three

The Noise of Them That Sing

Fundamental-ish Music

Five-point fundamentalism and other variations of neutrality share guilt for a national "Christian" acceptance of worldly and fleshly behaviors that have only recently been introduced to the churches. The personally disciplined life that recognizes charity's relationship to Christian liberty and offenses is the salt of the earth and light of the world responsible for holding back the tide of lukewarm toleration. The balance of this book will identify some specific pacifying accommodations embraced by some who still want to be known as independent Baptist fundamentalists.

Possibly the most volatile controversy among independent Baptists centers around the subject of Christian music. Because good men differ on what is acceptable and what is not, fireworks often result. These men are good men who preach the Gospel, who believe in the inspiration and preservation of Scripture, who believe in the deity, virgin birth, bodily resurrection and blood atonement of Jesus Christ. They are good men who align themselves with the fundamental independent Baptist movement of the twenty-first century.

Within the scope of beautiful music that can truly be classified as godly and holy is a wide gamut of preferences, from southern to symphonic, and a dozen genres in between. Within this realm of lovely music is abundant room for every believer to worship God without evoking the passions of the flesh or the displeasure of God. However, some of the differing of the aforementioned "good men" strays outside the allowances of preference into the territory of unspiritual music. When this happens, those "good men" who want to continue to align themselves with independent Baptist fundamentalism today say that music is a liberty matter for the individual believer or church, a gray area upon which God has no stated will.

However, if indeed all types of music fall under the category of Christian liberty for specific saints and particular churches, then all that has been stated earlier in this book about Christian liberty should be considered with regard to the music of both the home and the church. Again, if all the musical genres of our present day are liberty of the Christian, then music must pass the muster of Scripture, of charity and of offense.

music and the Word of God

"And the LORD said unto Moses, Go, get thee down; for thy people, which thou broughtest out of the land of Egypt, have corrupted themselves" (Exod. 32:7). Thus began the descent of Moses and Joshua from the smoke-enshrouded, fire-consumed height of Mt. Sinai, a rocky prominence of both geographical and spiritual significance to God's people, Israel. At the bequest of the people, Aaron had fashioned a god with the physical shape of a calf and the spiritual power of a devil. En masse, the people rose up early the morning after Aaron's proclamation of a feast to Jehovah and "offered burnt-offerings, and brought peace-offerings; and the people sat down to eat and to drink, and rose up to play" (vs. 6).

On the way down the rocky steeps of Mt. Sinai, Joshua heard the sound of revelry and debauchery at the base of the mountain. His untrained ears mistook the cacophonous, confusing noise for the chaotic conflict of war cries. Moses, more mature and informed by God, said, "It is not the voice of them that shout for mastery, neither is it the voice of them that cry for being overcome: but the noise of them that sing do I hear" (vs. 18).

The playing of the people in Exodus 32:6 was a mocking, scorning, sport-making activity that attracted God's displeasure and wrath to the extent He would have exterminated His people "had not Moses his chosen stood before him in the breach, to turn away his wrath, lest he should destroy them" (Ps. 106:23).

The playing of Exodus 32:6 was a religiously-approved, carnally-motivated deception that prompted the people to be "naked; (for Aaron had made them naked unto their shame among their enemies)" (vs. 25). The playing of Exodus 32:6 was a spiritual-sounding, offering-accompanied "worship" activity that God later revealed was idolatry: "Neither be ye idolators, as were some of them; as it is written, The people sat down to eat and drink, and rose up to play" (I Cor. 10:7).

The sound of the singing that Joshua mistook for the panic and fear of a military enemy's attack, Moses rightly described as the perversion and fun of a spiritual enemy's attack. In spite of the fact that the people felt in their hearts that God would be pleased with their offerings and their singing, the heart of God was righteously indignant with their utter forsaking of what He had already taught them. The word for "sing" in Exodus 32:18 is an uncommonly used word with a definition that includes the debasing of oneself through provocative, twisting gyrations. This singing was the type of music that would naturally accompany carnal expression and God had nothing good to say about it. So evil was this musical display that three thousand died at the hand of a God-authorized slaying of brothers and companions and neighbors throughout the camp of Israel!

Furthermore, God visited His people with a plague in which many more died. A commonly overlooked but heavily weighted truth from this Exodus passage is that it was the young, inexperienced ears of Joshua that were mistaken about the music. It was the older, seasoned ears of Moses that were clued in to the music. Obviously, age is not the only factor in discernment; however, age can be a factor. Just as clearly, experience is not the isolated condition upon which all right judgment is made; even so, experience is valuable in making right judgments.

Interestingly, most of the people who are sounding the trumpets about the world's new sound creeping into the churches are older and most of the people who are importing this new sound into the churches are younger. True, Joshua was sincere in what he thought he heard, and just as truly the younger believers are sincere in what they think they hear. Sadly, both Joshua and the younger, untrained ears of our day are wrong. It is high time for some of the importers of this trendy sound to consult with some of the Moses-types who can listen to five notes and say, "It is not the sound of spiritual battle against the forces of evil that I hear. No, what I am hearing is worldly, carnal, devilish music."

Existing in the world of music outside the ever-broadening boundaries of what is called Christianity—and to the shame of many inside—is a strange phenomenon. This phenomenon is manifested via many televised documentaries from groups interested in anthropology: the National Geographic Society, the Smithsonian Institution and others. Covered in many of these programs are the various customs of indigenous people groups from undeveloped nations. Invariably, the footage will feature video and audio recordings of the music of social and religious gatherings of these native tribes and clans.

What is of interest is that most of these undocumented, isolated and vanishing peoples have no consciousness of the vastness of the world outside their limited spheres. They have no information that other people exist in large nations. They certainly have never had contact with each other. After all, a vanishing tribal culture in the rain forest of the Brazilian Amazon has no means whatever of having contact or awareness of a similarly endangered primitive culture in the jungles of Borneo in Indonesia. A threatened people group in the interior of Africa possesses no ability of knowing of another disappearing tribe in the Australian outback.

Yet for all this inability of these groups to know anything about each other's existence, one similarity arises: their music. Regardless of the habitat of the particular region, these imaginative souls have skinned animals, stretched those skins over a rounded form, and fashioned primitive drums. These drums in turn have become the primary—often the only—instrument of accompaniment. Regardless of the racial origin of the specific group, the rhythm of the music is nearly identical: a syncopated thumping that accents the off-beat and diminishes the downbeat and creates agitation. Regardless of the unique characteristics of the particular people group being studied, the mood of the music is spiritually oppressing and sensually provocative.

While the music of these small tribes separated by vast oceans and living on different continents is uncannily the same, all their other customs and traditions are widely different, often having no similarity at all. Consider their ceremonial traditions, their adulthood initiations, their social interactions, their food-gathering methods, their preferred foods, their accepted attire, etc. When one realizes that most of these clans live in the tropical regions of the world, one cannot blame the differences upon climate. The differences are clearly due to individual ideas developed over centuries of time, accepted by the leadership and passed down to succeeding generations completely isolated from the influence of other cultures.

What must be explained is the reason that the lifestyles of these people groups are in such contrast in all areas except their music. The simple answer is that all around the world, pagan music has one author, and that author is the Devil. Additionally, Satan is no less the author of that music, whether it is played on a skin of a warthog boar stretched over a hollowed-out teak log or played on a thousand-dollar drum set on the platform of a multi-million-dollar mega-church. It defies logic that people who wear expensive jeans and drive sports cars and eat high-priced foods could dare to call such dissonance and noise "Christian music."

When the rock culture began to make slight inroads into the Neo-Evangelical community in the mid-twentieth century, independent Baptist fundamentalists decried this as "jungle music in the church house." While such a phrase would be considered racially insensitive in many settings in our present day, there is a reason that rock music was called jungle music. It resembles in its beat, mood and effect the music of pagans, a resemblance that is not accidental but by design of an evil, deceptive designer, Satan himself.

No one denies the profound influence that music exerts upon a culture or the strong impact that music possesses over hearers. For this reason and many others, independent Baptist fundamentalists must stop their flirtation and courtship with the music of the world and deny the inclination toward fundamental-ish music. This does not mean that all music sung or played in our churches must be at least a hundred years old. The age of the music is not the cause of debate. What is at issue is the kind of music that it is. God needs to be glorified, and Satan needs to be banished when the instruments are played and the voices are raised. Nothing less is acceptable.

Music, then is to be judged by God, not by man's heart. Neo-Evangelicalism supports rock, rap, country-western and hip-hop music as much as the world does. To the shame and reproach of the name *Baptist*, the name *Christian* and the concept of biblical fundamentalism, many independent Baptists are bending toward Christian music artists by accenting their worship services with the hip-hop twang and the nightclub scoop. God is just as displeased today with music that mixes pseudo-spirituality and semi-nudity and religious deviltry as He was thirty-five centuries ago.

Often, the compromiser's position is that music is amoral, having neither moral nor immoral potential or value. Five-point fundamentalists are cozying up to the Neo-Evangelicals on this matter more than they are standing with the founders of their independent Baptist churches and the forefathers of our faith. Out the door goes the objective commentary of God on the music of Israel's self-styled calf-worship festivities; in the door comes the subjective commentary of man. Out the door goes Moses' wisdom about this modern sound; in comes Joshua's naivety. New Evangelicals want the whole world to realize just how pure their hearts are at the "Christian rock" concert, just how real their worship is at the "Christian" rap show and just how close to God their adherents are at the "Christian" hip-hop festival. Refusing to admit or to confess that music can incite lustful as well as majestic responses, they replace the true praise of God with gross vulgarity, thus cheaply profaning the name of Jesus Christ.

While many fundamentalists would deny it, they are leading their churches and congregations just about ten years behind the very Neo-Evangelicals with whom they have the greatest disagreement on the subject of music. Forgotten in this demonstration is the fact that "the heart is deceitful above all things, and desperately wicked" (Jer. 17:9) and that only God knows "the hearts of all the children of men" (I Kings 8:39). Accompanying that forgetfulness is a centuries-old stubbornness that says, "We will walk after our own devices, and we will every one do the imagination of his evil heart" (Jer. 18:12). Neglected completely in this outward show of Corinthian Laodiceanism is Paul's Holy-Spirit-inspired statement, which says, "I judge not mine own self. For I know nothing by myself; yet am I not hereby justified: but he that judgeth me is the Lord" (I Cor. 4:3, 4).

Insistence that one's knowledge of his own heart's sincerity approves his music in God's eyes is flat defiance against the Lord who is the Judge of all. When the fundamentalist makes this his position, he is no more right than is the Neo-Evangelical.

His chanting of the mantras of independent Baptists does not make him right when his music is wrong. Deliberate posturing that one's totally subjective heart is the deciding factor as to the rightness of music is a categorical denial of what God says in His totally objective Scripture.

In Scripture, God has given His Word to judge all things. It is utter insanity that something as integral to worship as music would be without judgment. The Exodus reference is clearly enough to classify as evil all the modern genres of music "invented" since the moral revolution of the 1960s. What made a song unspiritual thousands of years ago makes it unspiritual today.

Every new style of music that has developed since the Beatles arrived in New York from Liverpool, blasphemously claiming more popularity than Jesus Christ, has the characteristics of that Mt. Sinai Music Festival of so long ago. Then and now the music is geared to the promotion of rebellion, prompting of nudity, pandering to self-gratification and perverting of spirituality.

It is not the time period in which a song is written that makes it spiritual or unspiritual. While the evil of every style of music that has been introduced since the 1960s has been mentioned, that is not to say that no spiritual music has been written in that same time period. Rather, the statement is that there has been no good new musical genre that has come about in that time period.

In addition to the music, the lyrics of the modern-sounding "Christian" songs are often shallow, inclusive, nebulous and at times profane. Many of the lines could be sung with equal application to Allah or Jehovah without the change of a single word. Added to that is a choreography that is licentious, lascivious, promiscuous, concupiscent chicanery that visually portrays a generation in love with debauchery. Altogether, it is a satanic door through which this generation has walked with its eyes closed in transcendental hypnosis of the spirit. Absolutely nothing of the music of this world can be classified as God-honoring, Christ-exalting or Holy-Spirit-filled.

The Exodus passage featuring Moses and Joshua is not the only passage in which God testifies of music as having moral qualities. Due to their similar content and message, the New Testament letters to the churches in Ephesus and Colossæ are often titled sister epistles. Both of these Books address the subject of the indwelling Holy Spirit's role in filling the believer. Among other things, this filling of the Spirit for surrendered biblical Christians is a factor in alert, circumspect living; in spiritual understanding of God's will; in proper temperance for one's life; in godly thanksgiving; in proper submission in all earthly relationships; in forbearance and forgiveness; in charitable living; in peace in one's heart; in reception of God's Word; and indeed, in whatever a person does as a believer. (See Ephesians 5:15–21; Colossians 3:12–17.)

In conjunction with these many other matters, both these epistles mention that the filling of the Spirit accompanies spiritual songs or that singing spiritual songs is one result of the Spirit-filled life. The idea in both instances is that Spirit-filled people will minister to one another in spiritual songs. As one present-day evangelist bluntly points out, the phrase "spiritual songs" proves the existence of unspiritual songs. If all songs were spiritual, the phrase "spiritual songs" would be as redundant as *dead corpse*. Obvious is the fact that some songs are unspiritual, and Spirit-filled people do not speak to others the words of those songs nor sing to others the tunes of those songs. The presence of a fundamentalist heritage and a sign promoting independence among Baptists does not guarantee the spirituality of the music from within.

The factors that make a song spiritual or unspiritual are its message, its messengers and its "messagees." The message is two-fold: words and music. The messengers are the writers, singers, performers and promoters. The "messagees" are those who buy it and listen to it.

When the musical or verbal message of a song promotes rebellion and unacceptable behavior, it is an unspiritual song. When the messengers are individuals or groups whose lives are largely lived in disharmony with the Bible's major doctrines and in disobedience with the Bible's major requirements, the music is an unspiritual song. When the "messagees" are primarily from the crowd that changes the Bible, humanizes Jesus Christ, profanes the Lord's Day, tolerates sin, decries holiness and promotes a general sloppiness of "Christianity," the music is an unspiritual song.

On the other side, the spiritual song will be a song with a message that is doctrinally accurate. Its messengers will live lives that are decidedly acceptable in light of Scripture. They will be divinely accountable to God both in private life and in public singing or playing. The "messagees" of spiritual songs will be deeply anchored to the unchanging God of the Bible by faith in Jesus Christ and by the fullness of the Holy Spirit.

The Lord's Supper hymn sung at the institution of the Lord's Supper, also called Communion or the Lord's Table, is another instance where biblical Christians can see the importance of music and indeed the right music. After eating and drinking with His disciples, the Lord Jesus Christ told them He would not eat or drink again with them until He did so in the kingdom. "And when they had sung an hymn, they went out into the mount of Olives" (Matt. 26:30).

WHAT HAD IMMEDIATELY PRECEDED THIS INSTITUTION OF THE LORD'S SUPPER WAS:

Jesus' anointing at the hands of Mary of Bethany

His preparations for His final
Passover meal with His disciples

His washing of the disciples' feet after
eating the Passover supper

An explanation of the symbolism of the elements of
unleavened bread and unfermented juice of the grape

His betrayal at the hands of a Satan-filled Judas Iscariot

WHAT IMMEDIATELY FOLLOWED WAS:

The grand Olivet discourse of John's fourteenth through sixteenth chapters

Jesus' high priestly prayer of John's seventeenth chapter

His agony in the Garden of Gethsemane

His capture by an angry mob armed with swords and staves

His mock trial at the hands of embittered religious leaders and corrupted political leaders

His substitutionary death and vicarious atonement for our sins

His glorious resurrection in victory over death and His restoration of a backslidden Peter

Perhaps the singing in Matthew 26:30 is not the only singing in which Jesus and His apostles engaged that evening, but it is the only singing mentioned in the record. And what did they sing? A hymn. It is unconscionable to purport that this hymn contained such lyric or music as would incite carnal passions, worldly pleasures or devilish palsies. It would be out of the context of both the events and mood of that sacred evening to suggest this hymn would produce dancing, hand-clapping, arm-swaying, body-convulsing or tongue-babbling. It would be unreasonable to teach that this hymn would contribute toward anything unholy or profane, anything indecent or unwholesome and anything inappropriate or questionable. It is indeed blasphemous to attempt to convince anyone that the hymn the disciples sang with Jesus Christ contained music and lyric that would coordinate piety with promiscuity, consecration with concupiscence or sanctification with sleaze!

The chosen song is reputed to have been one of the Hallel Psalms (113–118) sung by Jews the night prior to Passover for fourteen centuries prior and, incidentally, for the twenty centuries since. Nothing in the Scripture narrative indicates that a new song was written for the occasion; rather, everything about this Passover was observed just as it is written.

Everything about these six Psalms promotes the orderliness and sobriety and solemnity that characterize the worship of biblical Christians. Everything about these six Psalms contributes to the rejoicing and delight and praise that accompany the worship of biblical Christians.

GLORIOUS THEMES APPEAR
IN THESE SIX PSALMS:

Praise of God's name

Recognition of God's glory

Acknowledgement of God's uniqueness

Declaration of God's compassion

Remembrance of God's deliverance

Supremacy of God's person

Response to God's attention

Statement of God's righteousness

Preciousness of God's eternity and several more

Beautiful indications of Christ's suffering and death and resurrection appear throughout the six Psalms in consideration.

Prophecy and instruction

Praise and intercession

Preservation of saints and God's inclining to their cries

Paying of vows and insistence upon holiness, peace, prosperity and power

These concepts and more abound in these six Psalms. Nothing

in the six Psalms used by generations of the Hebrews for their Passover observances would promote the carnal Corinthianism of today's "Christian" rock, rap and hip-hop. Nothing in the six Psalms indicated as Hallel Psalms would cater to the worldly Laodiceanism of this culture's "Christian" contemporary worship. In fact, what these six Psalms show is completely exclusive of the type of "worship" made common by our sin-enthralled, compromising culture and being made normal by some still referring to themselves as fundamentalist brethren and churches.

The overall beauty and holiness and glory of our great God demands music that is just as beautiful and holy and glorious to celebrate Him. It is utterly degrading to God that any man would attempt to praise Him by means of the raunchy beat and discordant grinding of rock, the disturbing accents and mindless repetition of rap, the minor strains and depressing twang of country-western or the flippant caprice and arrogant thoughtlessness of hip-hop.

These styles of music have been for the last half-century associated with the lowest of people, the vilest of actions, the basest of morals, the loudest of rebellions, the worst of history and the devices of Satan. No biblical Christian would ever use these musical conveyances to attribute glory and praise to Jehovah God.

Amos, the herdsman-turned-prophet from Tekoa, stood firmly in the face of the musical genres of his day when he prophesied in the king's court under Jeroboam II. Said he,

> *"I hate, I despise your feast days, and I will not smell in your solemn assemblies.*

> *"Though ye offer me burnt offerings and your meat offerings, I will not accept them: neither will I regard the peace offerings of your fat beasts.*

"Take thou away from me the noise of thy songs, for I will not hear the melody of thy viols.

"But let judgment run down as waters, and righteousness as a mighty stream."—Amos 5:21–24.

He began his next chapter by saying, "Woe to them that are at ease in Zion," and proceeded to ask the nation of Israel if they considered themselves better than Calneh and Hamath and Gath and the kingdoms those cities represented. In other words, he was asking Israel if they thought they would escape judgment for doing the same things other nations did prior to judgment. Then, he made very plain who the people were to whom he preached and wrote:

"Ye that put far away the evil day, and cause the seat of violence to come near;

"That lie upon beds of ivory, and stretch themselves upon their couches, and eat the lambs out of the flock, and the calves out of the midst of the stall;

"That chant to the sound of the viol, and invent to themselves instruments of music, like David;

"That drink wine in bowls, and anoint themselves with the chief ointments: but they are not grieved for the affliction of Joseph"—6:3–6.

What a startling rebuke! And what a striking resemblance to the spiritual conditions characterizing the new musical movement that has found total acceptance among Neo-Evangelicals and is finding its way to acceptance among independent Baptists. No one could read these passages without realizing that the context is the worship of Israel, God's covenant people, who at that time in history were once again corrupt people. The mention of outward religious activities like observances, offerings and oblations in the cited portions makes this plain. Nor can anyone read these passages without understanding that the people thought they could mix with their worship of Jehovah God such carnalities and worldliness as music sung and performed with no judgment as to righteousness. Furthermore, they thought they could include in their worship of the Lord music played by people who were self-satisfied and unbothered by the contemporary cultural sins of gross hypocrisy, lackadaisical apathy and licentious revelry. This is precisely the musical condition of the "Christian" contemporary trend introduced in the 1970s, popularized in the 1980s, accepted wholesale by the New Evangelical mainstream by the 1990s and since then bought into and embraced by people who strangely want to still call themselves independent Baptists.

Amos spoke of the noise of the people's songs. The modern genres of music invented in the last half of the 1900s are noisy. The music is without melodious or harmonious beauty. The beat is disturbing and ominous. The vocalizations span the spectrum from screeching to seduction to sadness. These modern music styles—invented by people on drugs and booze, people in apostasy and rebellion, people of satanic and sensual bent—have popularized deafening volume. What can be said of this music of our generations in the United States can be said of the music of pagans the world over throughout history. However, what can be said of this music cannot be said of psalms, hymns and spiritual songs!

Every scriptural instance of the phrase "new song" refers to the new song of redemption and praise to our God in contrast to the old song of bondage and servitude to the world, the flesh and the Devil. When a soul trusts Christ as Savior, God gives him a new song. When that soul encounters various and sundry deliverances along the journey of faith, God gives him a new song.

This song is not new in the sense of modern versus outdated; it is new in the sense of the new spiritual life of faith versus the old life that was once dead in sins and helpless in bondage. Unsurprisingly, six of the nine references to the new song are found in God's hymnal, the Psalms. An examination of Psalms 33:1–4; 40:1–3; 96:1–14; 98:1–9; 144:9; and 149:1–9 will prove that the new song is a spiritual outgrowth of God's miraculous deliverance of the soul and that such new songs must never resemble the Egypt of any believer's experience prior to his salvation.

By definition, the new song of praise to God may be music or lyric or both. A biblical Christian may play solo piano or guitar or saxophone or any other instrument and glorify the Savior. A God-fearing believer may sing *a cappella* and glorify the Lord. A sanctified saint may also sing with instrumental accompaniment and glorify God. The cited verses from the Psalms prove the appropriateness of music or lyric or both in the worship of God's people.

One of the clever ploys of the contemporary, modern music scene is its insistence upon the separation of music (what is played) from lyric (what is sung). However, there is no Scripture that even hints at the idea that when both music and lyric are present, they are to be perceived as having separate messages. Furthermore, there is no Scripture that allows that when both music and lyric are present in a musical presentation, that the lyric has a message and the music does not (or vice versa).

At the dedication of Solomon's temple, "trumpeters and singers were as one, to make one sound to be heard in praising and thanking the LORD; and when they lifted up their voice with the trumpets and cymbals and instruments of musick, and praised the LORD, saying, For he is good; for his mercy endureth for ever: that then the house was filled with a cloud, even the house of the LORD; So that the priests could not stand to minister by reason of the cloud: for the glory of the LORD had filled the house of God" (II Chron. 5:13, 14). This passage shows that both music and lyric possess and communicate a message and it shows that the message must be one message.

The word "one" in verse thirteen carries the connotation of "united" or "alone." This indicates that the one sound was unity of the instruments and the voices united. Furthermore, when verse thirteen mentions their voice, not their voices, grammar proves that not only were the voices and the instruments in harmonious symphony, but the voices themselves were in such cooperative sound as to be one voice.

When given together, music and lyric affect each other, and it is here that Old and New Testament laws of clean and unclean come in. When the unclean touches the clean, the clean is made unclean. Never does the reverse occur. When unclean music is the vehicle for clean lyrics, the product is just as unclean as would be a message of blasphemy set to music from Handel's *Messiah*. Wrong music negates that property of praise and cancels any positive impact that message can have. The only way to avoid this fiasco is for both music and lyric to communicate the same message: the praise and glory of God.

Interestingly, when a true separatist is seeking to help a new or weaker believer to see the need to separate from the lost world's rock and rap and other unwholesome music styles because of the devilish lyrics, the new or weaker believer will often say, "Oh, I don't listen to the lyrics. I listen only to the music, man. It's the music that I need. Really, man, I don't even know the words." If, however, that Christian is seeking to help that new or weaker believer to see the need to separate from CCM and other world-approved, so-called "Christian" rock or rap because of the satanic, sensual beat, the response often is this: "Hey, man, I'm not even listening to the music. I'm into the words. Praise Jesus." Which way is it? It cannot be both ways.

This is an either-or matter, not a neither-nor matter or a whichever-way-works-for-me matter. The obvious effort is to justify music or lyric that have no place whatsoever in the audio-diet of biblical Christians.

Whenever music and lyric are together in passages about the new song, they are both communicating the same message, not unconnected messages. Repeatedly, the new song appears in a context in which God's child has been delivered. Delivered from what? Even a casual study of Scripture shows that the saints have been delivered from the "Egypts" of their various times in history, and God always says, "Ye shall henceforth return no more that way" (Deut. 17:16). That same general perusal of the Word of God demonstrates that the saints have been delivered from the flesh and they are to "make not provision for the flesh, to fulfil the lusts thereof" (Rom. 13:14). Again, that identical reading of the Bible will manifest that God's sons and daughters are delivered from Satan himself and are thus equipped to "stand against the wiles of the devil" and enabled "to withstand in the evil day" (Eph. 6:10, 12). The figurative bringing up out of the miry clay could be any number of things of the world, flesh or Devil. Certainly, such a deliverance was not accomplished by use of the music or lyric of the world, flesh or Devil, "for if Satan cast out Satan... how shall his kingdom stand?" (Matt. 12:26). David never used worldly, carnal or devilish music in his day, and neither should any of the people of God in this day.

The Book of the prophet Isaiah has been called a Bible in miniature with its first thirty-nine chapters corresponding to the thirty-nine books of the Old Testament and its last twenty-seven chapters paralleling the twenty-seven New Testament books.

This grand man with his infinitely grander Book addressed the new song in Isaiah 42:5–12 in several aspects.

First, note that with which Isaiah associated the new song: Creation, life, righteousness, comfort, preservation, light, the opening of blinded eyes, the freeing of prisoners, the Lord's unmatched name, the Lord's unshared glory, the Lord's unfailing prophecies and the Lord's unlimited reach to the ends of the world. Then, observe that which Isaiah separated from the new song he referenced: blindness, imprisonment, darkness and idolatry. The rock, rap, and be-bop-hip-hop crowd so favored by Corinthian and Laodicean believers in our day does not care if one believes in Creation or evolution; it does not concern itself with unrighteous life or living, does not limit itself to the one God of Scripture and does not have any plan to reach the unreached multitudes with the Gospel. Their main concern is money—money earned at the expense of the spirituality, morality and piety of deceived listeners. Not so with Isaiah! Not so with biblical Christians!

At the close of the canon of Scripture, God inspired His last-living, faithful apostle John to twice mention the new song (Rev. 5:1–10 and 14:1–5). In chapter five, the scene is the throne room of God and the seven-sealed book. In chapter fourteen, the context is the vision of the Lamb and the one hundred forty-four thousand Jewish evangelists who will preach the everlasting Gospel during the Tribulation period, thus bringing unnumbered multitudes to Christ.

Who could read these two passages without seeing that the new song is of the worthiness of Christ who has redeemed us out of the world, that the new song is about purity from the flesh and undefilement from the world, that the new song rings with the music and lyric of a thankful people toward a holy God? How, in the light of these many passages, can anyone propose to prove that worldly, sensual, devilish music and lyric is the new song of the saints? One wonders.

Understandably, some are asking why, if music is so important in our New Testament churches, are there so few New Testament references to songs and singing. This is a reasonable and honest question with a reasonable and honest answer. The New Testament was written to reveal things previously unrevealed in the Old Testament. On the subject of music, there was little more that needed to be said that had not already been stated in the words of the prophets in the years before Christ. Hence, there is precious little additional light on the subject. The Book of Acts says little and the epistles say little. God had already spoken concerning both acceptable and unacceptable musical expression.

As a matter of new truth, Paul did write, "I will sing with the spirit, and I will sing with the understanding also" (I Cor. 14:15). When a godly singer or Christ-honoring choir stands to sing "words easy to be understood" (vs. 9), every person in the listening audience can be edified. The words can be understood because they are sung melodiously, harmoniously and clearly in a rhythm that neither distracts nor defiles. When a carnal worldling swallows a microphone and shrieks out the words of a "Christian" rock song, only those who know the song can tell what is being said because the volume of the music and the distortion of the voice prevent anyone unfamiliar with the words from understanding them. Of course, I Corinthians, chapter fourteen, deals with the understanding of languages and the context is the tongues of the Corinthian church; but a simple application applies. Whether someone speaks an unknown language or a known language in an indecipherable manner makes no difference. Understanding comes only when the language is known and the pronunciation is perceived. No one can honestly say "Amen" at the end of a song if he has no idea what the singer(s) sang.

Late one night in Philippi, Paul and Silas sat in prison beaten, bloody, bound and likely blindfolded. "And at midnight, Paul and Silas prayed, and sang praises unto God" (Acts 16:25). God responded with a miraculous earthquake that opened prison doors and loosed prison shackles. God also responded with a miraculous restraint that kept all the prisoners from fleeing and with a miraculous deliverance in the salvation of the Philippian jailor and his family. All this came about as the consequence of prayer and singing of praises.

What kind of prayer was it? Was the prayer of Paul and Silas a worldly, sensual, devilish prayer? Had it been, God would have never answered with such amazing evidence of His pleasure. No more than the prayer could have been worldly, carnal or devilish could the singing have been worldly, carnal or satanic. Paul and Silas did not incorporate into their prayer some tavern song, some cutesy jingle from school-day concerts or some popular strain from the streets of Philippi. No. They sang praises to God that properly, beautifully, sincerely and faithfully complemented their prayer.

This chapter could delineate many other divinely inspired details regarding music, but one final, necessary thought concerns dancing. Because sensual, partially nude dancing is the norm in some of today's religious settings, the identity of the dance alluded to in Psalm 149:3 must be clear. This dance is just as much subjected to the requirement to glorify God as is music or lyric. David's dance and this dance are among the tiny number of dances to God mentioned in Scripture. The supposed should not ever eliminate the obvious in the understanding of such passages. What is obvious is that God was being glorified. What is just as obvious is that when the same Hebrew word for "dance" (gender changed only) is used in Exodus 32:19, God was not glorified. What was the difference? It was the *type* of dance, just as it is the type of music, the type of lyric and the type of performance. It was the accompanying and surrounding events of the dance, just like it is the accompanying and surrounding events of the music, lyric and performance!

Furthermore, it is profound that dancing is absolutely absent from the worship of the New Testament church in all the apostles' writings. The only dancing mentioned later in Scripture than Lamentations 5:15 is Herodias' daughter's sensual dance (Matt. 14:6; Mark 6:22), the father's celebratory dance (Luke 15:25), and the listener's unperformed dance (Matt. 11:17; Luke 7:32). To insist, then, that "Christian" dancing with its accompanying "Christian" rock and rap and twang is part of the worship of the church is to completely ignore the fact that Christ and the apostles never danced, that Paul never instructed any of the churches regarding the worship dance and that no worship passage of the New Testament includes the so-called "worship dance." To even hint that the vulgar gyrating, provocative body-bouncing, and defrauding semi-nudity of twenty-first-century "church worship dance" is permitted by God, to say nothing of approved by God, is utter denial of both the untouchable holiness and the glorious beauty of Jehovah God.

Truly, very few churches that identify themselves with the independent Baptist movement employ dancing. However, those churches that have introduced worldly music will eventually introduce worldly dancing.

While more passages about music could fill more pages of this book, it is important to tie the other two governing influences, biblical charity and the avoidance of offense, to the subject of the music of our churches. In the realm of music, the issue of whether or not one is displaying charity becomes rather subjective and nebulous because a person can *say* he is filled with the Spirit, whether he is or isn't. He can say his music edifies others, whether it does or doesn't. He can say his music will meet the qualifications of the list in I Corinthians 13, whether it will or won't.

However, the matter of offense is not subjective at all. The matter of whether music offends is clearly measurable and observable by the fruit of that music, by the results of that music, by the verifiable revival or lack thereof in those who perform the music, listen to the music and approve the music. Many compromising moderns do not see true Heaven-sent, Holy-Ghost prompted revivals because they are attempting to force the hand of God instead of crying out for God to move His own hand. Several pragmatic believers are missing God-wrought, life-altering, church-transforming, New-Testament revivals due to the fact that they are expecting God to open the prison doors and save Philippian jailors to the music of the world with a few Jesus lyrics plugged in.

Some fundamentalists will say that they are not playing music of rebels with Jesus lyrics plugged in. They will say that they are not playing the music of the "Christian" contemporary music (CCM) sound, the music of the mega-parachurch movements, or the music of the non- and inter-denominational crowds. And to their credit, they are right. They are not using that music…yet. *Yet* is the operative word.

However, some who still call themselves independent Baptists, who still want to say they are fundamentalists, who still want to keep their fellowship secure, are flirting with the CCM-mega-parachurch-non-and inter-denominational music.

This flirtation is like all flirting. Flirting is not commitment, but it is an open door to it. The absence or presence of flirtation is one characteristic separating spiritual courtship from humanistic dating.

It is an overture, no pun intended, to the CCM sound and the mega-parachurch groups and the non- and inter-denominational crowd, when an otherwise strong, independent Baptist (individual or church) decides to borrow music and "rewrite the score." The argument of some is that by changing the underlying rhythm in a few spots and by re-timing the chorus a bit and by rewriting a couple lines to clarify doctrine, an unspiritual song can be turned into a spiritual song. None of this effectively effaces the association of the song, indeed the origin of it, with which most people in the audiences will be familiar.

A song written by Martin Luther in the sixteenth century has an origin in Lutheran theology, but the time lapse of half a millennium has completely disassociated that song from his beliefs. As proof, it is clear that no one has been led into covenant theology or Calvinism by singing, "A Mighty Fortress Is Our God." However, when an avowed compromiser, a known Neo-Evangelical or an outright apostate who is still living wrote a song in 2010 and the fundamentalists are using that song "with minor changes" within the decade, that song is absolutely associated with that person, with his doctrine, with his religious affiliations, with his lifestyle and with everything about him. Strangely, the same church that will scrutinize its Bible conference speakers and revival speakers and missionary speakers for their doctrinal stand will flirt with music written and sung by people whose doctrinal stand is far from Baptist or biblical!

This serves as an occasion of offense. Lost sinners and weak saints alike know what is going on in the world of music. Every avenue of social media continually bombards the audio-senses. Having little or no biblical basis for decision-making, they have melded with their generation. The world's music is their music. When those lost sinners walk into a Bible-preaching church and hear a song that has been varied just a bit, the message is this:

"Clean up your life a little bit, and God will accept you." When a Neo-Evangelical compromiser walks into a Bible-preaching church and hears a song that has been altered just a little, the message is clear: "We borrow from the world to be relevant." To both, the message is clear: "We don't want to be righteous over much" (See Ecclesiastes 7:16).

The lost person who believes he needs to clean up a little may actually do that, but he will be just as lost as he was before. He can empty and sweep his house and still be a lost sinner. The weak believer who thinks that Christianity is just a slight adaptation of the world can adapt a little and still be just as carnal and worldly as before. By giving people such false assurances, some who want to identify as fundamentalists are actually helping the downfall of righteousness and godliness and holiness in music, and thus helping the downfall of independent Baptist fundamentalism.

Indeed, if one considers the biblical definition of offenses, five-point fundamentalists who are borrowing from the world are guilty of wounding the weak consciences of young believers and emboldening the dead consciences of pagan sinners. Their reaching across the boundary to be relevant to this generation is their failure to let the reproaches of Christ fall upon them. Of course, the five-point fundamentalist knows the right doctrine. Unfortunately, all too often, in his accommodations to Neo-Evangelical music, he forgets that "there is not in every man that knowledge." Unfortunately, all too often, in his insistence that he is doing more good than harm, his "knowledge puffeth [him] up" (I Cor. 8:1, 7).

As to the words and their vehicle of expression, compromising fundamentalists would increasingly have us believe that the musical accompaniment is irrelevant as long as the words are true. How different was the position and practice of our Savior! The

Gospels of Mark (1:24) and Luke (4:34) both record for us that in the synagogue of Capernaum was a man with an unclean spirit. This man spoke the truth about Jesus Christ: "I know thee who thou art, the Holy One of God." The message was true, but the mouthpiece was devilish. The message was true, but the vehicle to communicate that message was devilish. Jesus' response was not passive or tolerant, although the man was a "good advertisement" for the Messiah. His response was active rebuke. He told this devil to hold his peace. He silenced the devil, not because the message was wrong or bad but because the means of communication was motivated from beneath, even from Hell itself.

Another Scripture portion that emphasizes this concept is Acts 16:16–18 where Paul and Silas and Timothy had just unpacked their travel bags at the house of Lydia prior to the hour of prayer. As they left her house to assemble at the place of prayer, "a certain damsel possessed with a spirit of divination met" them and followed them crying out, "These men are the servants of the most high God, which shew unto us the way of salvation."

Her message was doctrinally correct. Her message was spiritually true. Her message was culturally helpful. Her message was personally kind.

However, it was not the words but the vehicle of her words that caused Paul to be grieved in his spirit enough to turn and command the devil, a spirit of divination, to depart from her that hour.

The psalmist noted this exact issue in Psalm 50:16–23 where he stated, "Whoso offereth praise glorifieth me: and to him that ordereth his conversation aright will I shew the salvation of God" (vs. 23). What is notable is that the passage begins in verse 16 with a soul-searching question: "But unto the wicked God saith, What hast thou to do to declare my statutes, or that thou shouldest take my covenant in thy mouth?" Thievery, adultery, deceit and slander—these are cited as rendering "praises" null and void. Those who do not order their conversations aright are disqualified mouthpieces for the message of glory to Jehovah God. Psalm 144:8 and 11 also addresses the type of praise given by those whose mouths speak vanity and hands perform falsehood as part of the reason for spiritual declension. The new song, however, would help sons and daughters grow into godly adults, help bring about social prosperity and help ensure peace within the streets (vss. 12–15).

Such discrimination in sizing up lyric and music is in order today. When the "stars" of "Christian" rock and rap clearly espouse false doctrine, why do they have the access to fundamental churches and pulpits? When the songwriters and singers, the authors and artists and the creators and communicators of this new music are sympathetic toward multi-versionism, Lordship salvation, hyper-Calvinism, religious humanism, non-scientific evolution and a long shopping list of other heresies, why do the so-called fundamentalists want to "just rewrite a note or two and sing the song right"? When the performers of CCM are understanding of and tolerant of and even supportive of sinful lifestyles, why do they have the *carte blanche* underwriting of some of our five-point fundamentalist brethren? It's simple. More and more claim that music is a gray area, an area where believers have rights to individual preference, an area in which the saints have far broader liberty than scriptural statutes allow.

Seemingly, as long as a popular person is shouting something about Jesus, compromisers are happy. A professional athlete who prays is the hero of the compromisers even while missing church to play his sport on Sunday. A movie star who claims to be a person of faith is immediately placed upon a compromiser's pedestal, even if his movie roles demean the Scripture, the family, the church, or holiness or decency in general. Just as the damsel with the spirit of divination spoke a true statement, some contemporary artists and promoters speak some truth. Just as this girl was well-known in the prosperous town of Philippi, many rock and rap CCM artists are famous around the world. Just as the young woman was influential, so are many of the modern vocalists and songwriters. However, when the vehicle for the message is an evil spirit—and no spiritually-discerning soul can deny the obvious connection between devils and "the noise" of them that sing modern musical types—that evil spirit must be cast out. Would to God that a generation of Spirit-filled young persons would arise and rebuke the devils of rebellion and immorality that infiltrate every note of rock, rap, country-western, hip-hop and whatever other genres of this world's music will be marketed to this and to the next unsuspecting generation(s)!

The singer is not the sole mouthpiece for a song. The actual music and the method of playing the instrument is also a communicator. The words of the prophet echo this matter:

"Take thou away from me the noise of thy songs, for I will not hear the melody of thy viols.

"But let judgment run down as waters, and righteousness as a mighty stream."

"That chant to the sound of the viol, and invent to themselves instruments of musick like David."—Amos 5:23, 24; 6:5.

The wrong kind of music indicates a lack of good judgment and an absence of righteousness. The right kind of music would replace the wrong kind if honest, sincere scriptural discernment were employed and if godly, holy righteousness were present. Obviously, it is not the instruments themselves with which God is displeased. The instrument is simply the tool.

Rather, it is the way the instrument is employed or played. David is not being castigated here for inventing instruments; neither are the people of Israel in Amos' day being chided for developing or manufacturing instruments. Rather, the reproof is against the use of good instruments for bad purposes. The same instrument can play psalms of worship or pseudo-worship, hymns or honky-tonk, spiritual songs or seductive songs. Amos 6:5 appears in context of age-of-Noah apathy with regard to sin.

chapter four

The Unmentionable Abomination

Fundamental-ish Attire

Independent Baptist preachers have gained the honorable reputation of preaching the full counsel of God, including the less-pleasant subjects known as abominations—most of the abominations, that is. Especially in the new millennium, one of them has become the unmentionable abomination among altogether too many independent Baptists.

The word *abomination,* in its varied forms, appears one hundred seventy-six times in Scripture; if averaged, one of every six and one-half chapters of the Bible mentions something abominable. An abomination is an expression or a behavior strongly disapproved of by God, and by extension, by godly people. Indeed, some of the strongest language in the entire Bible is expressed in context with abominations.

The bulk of references to abominable things concerns that which is abominable to the unchanging God of Creation. While it may seem superfluous, in this day of licensure and toleration it must be stated that any idea, expression or behavior that was abominable to the Lord at some time in history is still abominable to Him because He is immutable. His likes and dislikes do not change with the cultures!

The abominations against God detailed in the Scripture are found in three distinct categories: spiritual, moral and ethical. Abominations against God of the spiritual category include all forms and practices associated with idolatry, all profaning of offerings and polluting of the name or the house of the Lord, the practicing of any type of witchcraft and pride that governs the heart and results in general or specific rebellion against any direct commandment of the Lord.

Abominations against the Lord of the moral category include every deviant and perverted sexual behavior that the sinful mind can conjure. In specific, God identifies fornication, adultery, sodomy, incest, cross-dressing, bestiality, murder, all degrees and extents of lying and deceit and the sowing of discord against and disregard for divinely-ordained leadership.

By extension, vile habits in which base souls engage as they commit abominations would also be abominable.

The category of abominations against Jehovah dealing with ethical matters is the smallest category in the Word of God, being primarily comprised of business fraud, oppression of or extortion of the poor, false testimony that condemns the guiltless or frees the guilty and so forth.

The unmentionable abomination is a moral one, the one regarding cross-dressing that addresses distinction between men's clothing and women's clothing.

> "The woman shall not wear that which pertaineth unto a man, neither shall a man put on a woman's garment: for all that do so are abomination unto the LORD thy God."—Deut. 22:5.

the obvious

Sanctified attire has always been a distinctive mark of the separated, godly people of biblical Christianity. From the earliest times dating forward to the apostles, and then from the apostles to this present day, all existing documentation on the subject supports a modest, gender-distinguishing clothing style among the saints. Indeed, consecrated believers have ever been chaste in their choices of clothing. Whatever styles the world may have foisted upon the unsuspecting and the uncaring of any generation or culture have been carefully weighed by godly believers prior to those said godly believers wearing those said styles.

Written records of the people of God (for example, the Separatists, also known as Pilgrims) attest to the modest ladylike attire of women as being completely different garments than the most manlike attire of men.

Written sermon material from the times of the founding fathers of our land would attest to the modesty and distinction with which Christian gentlemen and Christian ladies attired themselves.

The earliest photographic evidence in which Christians are the subject shows men and women in distinctly different attire; moreover, they were covered modestly and appropriately. It was not until the sexual revolution of the latter half of the twentieth century had plowed and harrowed American culture that believers stooped to embrace uni-gender apparel and immodest appearance.

Any clothing style that flaunts and shows off rather than complements, covers and conceals is not only suspect but is decidedly wrong. While the less-concerned among believers have adapted to the fashion of the season, believers who are devoted to

Christ have not. Independent Baptists are among the last to stop talking about this unmentionable abomination and the results are the same as they were when the Neo-Evangelicals stopped talking about this subject preserved decades ago.

The issues of modesty and gender-distinction are admittedly subjective in nature. What is modest to one person may not be to another. What is distinctly masculine or feminine to this believer may not be to that one. For that reason alone, one must refer to an objective set of criteria to determine what God says is modest and distinct with regard to the man and the woman.

Peter's clear teaching regarding a godly lady's outward adorning is that it must be in step with "that which is not corruptible, even the ornament of a meek and quiet spirit, which is in the sight of God of great price" (I Pet. 3:5). An ornament is a visible representation of the tastes of the wearer.

The clothing, jewelry, hairstyle and all other visible manifestations of a woman reflect the "hidden man of the heart" that men cannot see. As is so common with God, He requires that what cannot be seen be honestly and unmistakably represented by what can be seen.

Paul's equally lucid command regarding a godly lady's attire and appearance is that it must be "modest apparel, with shamefacedness and sobriety... (which becometh women professing godliness)" (I Tim. 2:9). The verb "becometh" is the operative word. This word means that her modest apparel— literally loose, flowing clothing—worn with shamefacedness (bashfulness) and sobriety (self-control) would be complementary to, not contradictory to, a profession of godliness. "Shamefacedness" refers to bashfulness or a casting down of the eyes, and "sobriety" speaks of self-control and soundness of mind. This requirement that a woman's outward attire be becoming to a profession of godliness would be ludicrous unless it were also possible for a woman to wear clothing that would be unbecoming to a profession of godliness.

These New Testament apostolic guidelines are not isolated rantings; rather, they are fuller developments of the teachings of the Lord Jesus Christ Himself who said,

> *"Think not that I am come to destroy the law, or the prophets: I am not come to destroy, but to fulfil.*
>
> *"For verily I say unto you, Till heaven and earth pass, one jot or one tittle shall in no wise pass from the law, till all be fulfilled."—* Matt. 5:17, 18.

How strange, yet not so strange really, that Jesus said just moments later,

> *"Ye have heard that it was said by them of old time, Thou shalt not commit adultery:*
>
> *"But I say unto you, That whosoever looketh on a woman to lust after her hath committed adultery with her already in his heart."—* Vss. 27, 28.

One would need contortionist's calisthenics to get out of this verbal grip of Christ. He obviously was stating that as long as Heaven and earth (both still present as of this writing) stand, the eternal, moral law to which He referred would still have bearing upon righteousness and godliness. Furthermore, He was absolutely relating the sin of actually committing adultery with what a man looks upon. In addition, He was implying that when a man looks upon a woman attired such that she stirs his lusts, her seduction is revealed in measure equal to his whoremongering.

Equally and necessarily true is the unstated fact that when a man looks upon a woman attired such that she draws his admiration and respect, her heart of godliness, meekness, quietness, shamefacedness, and sobriety is just as much revealed as is his heart of purity and integrity and decency!

In returning to Deuteronomy 22:5 as an Old Testament command on the subject of modesty and gender-distinction, it is sensible to state that no simpler verse exists in which God covers the topic of modest gender-distinct apparel. For all the modern attempts to explain away this verse, for all the arguments about this verse, and for all the attacks against this verse, one would think God has required that His saints wear torturous and ridiculous clothing. In actuality all God expects is decency and distinction.

the objections

Objections to the use of Deuteronomy 22:5 abound. The time was when the compromising Neo-Evangelicals were actually the spokespeople for these objections. Today, Neo-Evangelicals are as steeped in worldliness as the modernists and atheists; they do not even speak to this subject. Today, the independent Baptists are weakly raising the objections, or worse yet, falling silent.

THE "DONE-AWAY" OBJECTION. Perhaps the most often-heard objection to Deuteronomy 22:5 as a judgment regarding men's and women's attire in our generation is the tired "done-away" argument. Those who hold this position state that Deuteronomy 22:5 is part of God's law system that was done away in Christ.

This is problematic because only three distinct types of law or commandment can be scripturally placed on the "done-away list." The first division of "done-away" law is priesthood law which was changed because the priesthood changed (Heb. 7:12–17). Old

Testament believers under Mosaic Law approached God via the priesthood of Levi with Aaron and his direct-line descendants as priests and high priests. New Testament believers come to the throne of grace under the priesthood of Melchisedec with Jesus Christ as the great High Priest and all believers as priests under Him. Deuteronomy 22, however, is not a passage about priests or priesthood. Therefore, the change of priesthood law does not apply to Deuteronomy 22:5.

The second portion of "done-away law" is the Jew-versus-Gentile law which was abolished. Ephesians 2:14 and 15 call this Jew-versus-Gentile law "the middle wall of partition between us" and "the law of commandments contained in ordinances." A full exploration of Ephesians 2:11–16, Colossians 2:10–17, Colossians 3:11 and Acts 15:8–21 will conclusively prove the abolition of the Jew-Gentile distinctions which were required only under the Mosaic system.

The key is to distinguish between what is abominable to the Lord and what is abominable to a particular people group or ethnic culture. Genesis 29:26 cites a tradition that would have been abominable in ancient Syrian culture. Genesis 43:32 and 46:34 cite a specific matter that would have been abominable to the pagan Egyptians. Leviticus, chapter 11, and Deuteronomy, chapter 14, detail foods and living styles that were to be held in abomination among the ancient Hebrews but not among other peoples. Clearly Deuteronomy 22:5 is not a Jew-Gentile distinction because its abomination clause does not limit the subject of the verse to the Jew-Gentile division. The abomination clause in that verse speaks of an abomination to the Lord, not of an abomination to the Jew.

The third classification of "done-away law" concerns the death penalty. Christ became a curse for us and redemption in

Jesus Christ delivers New Testament believers from that curse according to Galatians 3:13. The death penalty in New Testament times is not the responsibility of Christians individually, nor is it the duty of Christians collectively under the auspices of the church. The church is not New Testament Israel. The New Covenant in the blood of Jesus Christ places the death penalty for sins and crimes fully into the jurisdiction of human governments (Romans 13 and I Peter 2).

Deuteronomy 22:5 is not death-penalty law; no commandment for stoning is connected to it.

PRIESTHOOD OBJECTION. Another popular objection to using Deuteronomy 22:5 to address contemporary dress standards is that the verse is a priesthood restriction. Because the Levitical priesthood made no provision for female priestesses, and because Deuteronomy, chapter 22, lacks any contextual tie to priests or the priesthood, this objection fails even a surface investigation. It is dishonest Bible study to connect a verse to a subject when the subject is not mentioned in the context. The closest references to priests are in Deuteronomy 21:5 where they are the investigators of an unsolved murder and in Deuteronomy 24:8 where they are investigators of the plague of leprosy.

ROBE OBJECTION. Proponents of this objection like to announce that everyone wore robes in Old Testament times so everyone now can wear pants or whatever else becomes the fad in the next decade or half-century. This is an erroneous—not to mention amusing—conclusion, in consideration of the robes listed and mentioned in Scripture. Of the thirty-seven references to robes found in all of God's Word, not one of those references even closely indicates that a robe was everyday attire for either men or women, to say nothing of the robe being a common, unisex garment worn by godly people in the homes, marketplaces, businesses and workplaces of their respective societies throughout history.

Priests' robes were symbols of glory and beauty worn only during ministry in the tabernacle or temple (Exod. 28, 39). Kings' robes were specific garments symbolic of royalty and authority but not worn by the populace for everyday use (I Sam. 24:4–11; I Kings 22:10, 30; I Chron. 15:27; Isa. 22:21). Interestingly, when Ahab was seeking to deceive the Syrians by disguising himself in battle, he told Jehoshaphat to dress in a royal robe for the battle. Obviously, a robe was not common battle attire. The wearing of a robe on a battlefield would immediately identify Jehoshaphat as a king because it was not common, everyday attire for a man, not even a king. Multicolored robes were symbols of the virginity and innocence of a king's daughter (II Sam. 13:18) but were certainly not every day wear for other men's daughters, to say nothing of the citizenry in general.

Micah 3:8 references a cape-like outer garment, a protective robe that would shield from cold, from sandstorms, or from thorns and briers. This particular flowing outer garment, comparable to today's western overcoat, cannot be cited as approved by God as a unisex garment for both genders.

The "best robe" for the prodigal, a symbol of celebration and restoration, (like a tuxedo today), was certainly not an everyday item of apparel (Luke 15:22). Pharisees' robes were symbols of self-righteousness (20:46) and were denounced by the Lord Jesus Christ as such. Christ's robe, a symbol of His deity (Isa. 22:21; Rev. 7:9), is unique and not comparable to any others. Finally, robes of righteousness for the saints (Job 29:14; Isa. 61:10; Rev. 6:11) are figurative in reference to our earthly sojourn, becoming literal attire only upon glorification in Heaven.

Never in the record of God's Word is a robe described as

daily attire. Artist's renditions have led us to think that robes were daily attire, but much art is inaccurate, unacceptable and even pornographic. Perhaps this is the reason that God told His people to destroy the pictures left behind by abominable and spiritually destitute cultures (Num. 33:52). We would be the wiser to let the Scripture teach us art and not the reverse.

ABSENCE OF WORDS OBJECTION. Related to the previous objection is this one, namely, that mention of our modern-day dresses, skirts and pants is virtually absent in Scripture. Instead of citing specific clothing articles, God expressed a truth that could transcend both generational change and cultural uniqueness. How wise of God to speak of "that which pertaineth to a man" and a "woman's garment" because these phrases apply to all time.

By definition, if there is clothing that pertains to a man, there is also clothing that pertains to a woman. If no clothing exists that pertains to a woman in any given generation and culture, the mention of clothing that pertains to a man in any given generation and culture is moot and irrelevant.

By definition also, if there is a woman's garment, there is also a man's garment. If no garment exists that is a man's garment in any given generation or culture, the mention of a woman's garment in any given generation or culture is equally moot and irrelevant.

While God does not mention pants or dresses or skirts in this context, breeches are mentioned in Scripture and always for men. The use of the word *skirt* in Scripture is nearly always connected in some way to protection. Ruth 3:9 records Ruth's request for Boaz to spread his skirt, his protective ability, over her. The context proves she was presenting herself as willing to be his wife although he was much older than she. First Samuel 24:4, 5 and 11 refer to the skirt of Saul's robe, a hem that protected the entire garment from unraveling. Not surprisingly, girls who dress in modest skirts and dresses are protected from men's leering glares and sensual advances much more than are their counterparts who wear tight jeans.

The origin of pants and overalls on women in Rosie the Riveter's World War II advertisements and in Hollywood's The Devil Is a Woman (1935) is a shaky foundation upon which to justify a Christian female's wearing of pants. Incidentally, Hollywood announced that movie starring Marlene Dietrich as its introduction of cross-dressing to American society. Fad and fashion may have blurred the lines, but pants still pertain to a man while skirts and dresses still pertain to a woman.

The introduction of earrings, necklaces and bracelets for the male gender is also paving the way for the social acceptance of feminine apparel, including skirts, hose and other apparel, on males. Even in this modern age of tolerance, a male in a skirt or dress is still called a cross-dresser. How much longer society will recognize that is quite uncertain. How soon it will be that such individuals are no longer called cross-dressers remains to be seen. Regardless of fad and popular notion, there are men's and women's distinct garments and believers who fail to recognize that are contributors to the epidemic of gender confusion.

MILITARY OBJECTION. A fourth objection is one that has only recently arisen. This newly discovered "scholarly idea" is that Deuteronomy 22:5 applies to military uniforms. The context of the chapter never mentions the military; furthermore, the Hebrew army had no female recruits or officers. All the censuses for war involved men twenty years of age and upward. Stating that this verse is a prohibition of women donning men's army uniforms does not address the second prohibition of the verse, that of a man putting on a woman's garment. This objection falls apart due to its lack of contextual reference, its lack of grammatical substantiation and its lack of simple logic.

Incidentally, why didn't any of the Bible scholars in the 1700s see this and forbid women's involvement in the War for Independence from 1776 to 1783? Why didn't any of the scholarly commentators of the 1800s understand this and preach against women on battlefields in the Civil War from 1861 to 1865? Why didn't any of the great preachers of the first half of the 1900s understand this and speak against women's presence in the First World War from 1914 to 1918 and the Second World War from 1938 to 1945? To all these queries, one can answer that this verse has nothing to do with soldiers. Additionally, the lion's share of photographic evidence of women's involvement in these wars shows them in long, flowing garments, whether civilian or otherwise.

TEMPERATURE OBJECTION. Another protest regarding the wearing of skirts and dresses by women is the "climate complaint". In essence, this objection is incredulously expressed by exasperated and frustrated women's libbers who ask with an eye roll if God expects women to freeze to death when the temperature is below zero.

In the hope that the reader will indulge the writer, the author will give a personal testimony of his late grandmother, Bessie Farnham (1891–1987), who lived her entire ninety-six years of life in northern Vermont. Married to an uncouth and ungodly man, she maintained her ladyship in spite of her husband's coarseness, the demands of farm chores, the lack of indoor plumbing for two-thirds of her life, and yes, the cold. Northern Vermont is home to bitter winter blasts of arctic air from the Hudson Bay that bring December and January temperatures into the thirties and forties below zero Fahrenheit not including wind chill.

In all her years of life, including more without running water than with it, she never wore pants. In all her outdoor chores, including milking by hand in an unheated stable, she never wore pants. In all her hardships in those many winters, she wore dresses, and in the three decades that this author knew his grandmother prior to her passing, no word ever crossed her lips of the advantage she would have if she could have worn overalls. Even though she lived well past the time when pants on women became the accepted norm, she never even thought of it.

the obligations

Believers today have several obligations in relationship to this subject.

IMPORTANCE OBLIGATION. The first obligation of any serious believer is to consider the weight of the clause, "for all that do so are abomination to the LORD thy God." God is saying something important when He speaks of an abomination. This is similar phrasing used to express God's strong aversion to idolatry (I Kings 11:5–7), pride, lying, murder (Prov. 6:16–19), sodomy (Lev. 18:22) and stealing (Prov. 11:1). The concept of cross-dressing between the genders is so bad that it is classified along with these sins as an abomination to our Lord. For independent Baptists in the twenty-first century to abandon this verse as having nothing to do with believers' clothing under grace is to ignore the obvious in favor of the frivolous.

Many have been heard to say that this verse is not an important command, because Jesus Christ said the two main commandments were to love God with all one's heart, soul, mind and strength and to love one's neighbor as himself (Matt. 22:35–40). The same Lord Jesus Christ also said that any man who would break one of the least commandments and teach others to do so would be called least in the kingdom of Heaven (5:17–19).

Even if this is the least commandment in all of God's Word, to break or to teach others to break, whether in word or by example, it puts that person down to the bottom of God's list in the kingdom of Heaven. The "abomination clause" connected with this commandment precludes its being one of the least commandments. Even though our Lord Jesus never disclosed what the least commandment is, it would logically stand to reason that the least commandments would have no abomination clause or sharp penalty connected to them. Again, it behooves twenty-first-century independent Baptist fundamentalists to look long and hard at what the actual abomination of this verse is and to avoid it.

SCHOLARSHIP OBLIGATION. Another obligation incumbent upon twenty-first-century saints is study. Very often, conversations about this verse degenerate into what the verse does not mean rather than move toward what it does mean. Telling what a verse does not mean while omitting or refusing to explain what it does mean is very poor Bible scholarship and is unacceptable for one attempting to rightly divide the word of truth. Knowing what is not meant along with what is meant is the safe and true way to study Scripture. Many who seem satisfied to rely upon what they think this verse does not mean would not rest easy with the same study method of other verses.

Consultation with commentaries written by respected, godly men from the time of the translation of the King James Bible all the way to 1950 will include the fact that Deuteronomy 22:5 prohibits immodesty and cross-dressing between the genders of God's people. Why should believers in the twenty-first century discredit centuries of godly scholarship and the agreed understanding of this verse?

REALITY OBLIGATION. Clamoring voices of our culture are all about gender equality. Truthfully, the genders are not equal. They are unique and their value to each other lies in full respect for and acceptance of those unique qualities. It is an utter denial of reality to turn one's back on this undeniable truth. Reality remains, whether it is admitted or respected or not. This is not an anti-man or anti-woman position; rather, this is pro-man and pro-woman. This is recognition of the uniqueness and specialness of each gender—the proper masculinity and prowess of men as well as the beautiful loveliness and mystique of women. This is respect for men in appropriate recognition of their strength and work; furthermore, it is respect for women in the shamefacedness of modesty that defines them as ladies.

COURAGE OBLIGATION. Independent Baptists are the last standing regiment of Bible believers who even speak of this issue. Many are the pastors and evangelists who have become discouraged with heartless ultra-legalism on one side and pitiful lasciviousness on the other. They have watched as the former soldiers of the cross one by one pull down their colors. Many who once stood for gender-distinction and modesty never mention it any more. Pastors fear losing members and givers. Revivalists fear losing meetings. Parents fear losing the "friendship" of their children. The need of the hour is courage.

AVOIDANCE OF OFFENSE OBLIGATION. New Testament independent Baptists in today have an obligation to avoid offense. Form-fitting garments all draw attention to a woman's figure. While skirts and dresses can be loose and flowing, most pants designed for women are seductively tight and alluringly cut. Fashion designers unashamedly admit that the pants they manufacture for women are for the purpose of turning men's heads.

the observations

God has made the attire of men and women a spiritual matter; a worldly and carnal society has turned it into a fashion/fad matter. In truth, many do not arrange their lives around their faith and the truth of God; instead, they cleverly arrange their faith and selected truths around their lives, while omitting other truths which do not fit or might upset their lifestyles. Fashion, vogue, the times and the weather dictate attire for them, but God does not.

From its earliest roots in 1607 until about 1960 (350 years), this nation stood as a stark testimony to the Lord that there is a definite boundary of modesty and an equally definite distinction between men's and women's clothing.

Then, immodesty and similar clothing was introduced and accepted for men and women. About 1960, both genders began dressing in degradingly skimpy clothing. At the same time, women began dressing like men. Men began growing long hair like women, thus removing the clear appearance distinction.

Around 1980, the next generation of men and women began engaging in same-gender lust, thus removing the activity distinction. A third generation which began around 2000 saw the complete removal of the acceptance distinction, and now our culture accepts alternate lifestyles and condemns the righteous.

The most recent development in this drain-circling decay of our culture is the United States Supreme Court decision in June 2015 which legalized marriage between persons of the same gender. In short, those who muddy the waters of modesty and gender distinction in our day are considered far less dangerous than are fundamental, Bible-believing Christians. Today, in shockingly accurate fulfillment of Romans 1:18–32 and II Timothy 3:1–8, our nation is more Roman and Greek than Puritan or Pilgrim, to say nothing of Separatist and Baptist!

The Christian individual who dresses modestly and distinctively to his or her gender has never, by so doing, led someone else into wrong thinking or actions. That being said, one must ask what has happened to the attitude that says, *If my clothing makes my brother to offend, I will not wear this again while the world stands.* No adolescent young man who dresses in keeping with his pure manhood and no adolescent young lady who dresses in keeping with her innocent womanhood has ever influenced someone else into impure imaginations, into troubling and tempting thoughts or into lewd and lascivious licentiousness. That being stated, one must ask himself how so many justify their conciliatory stance toward worldly and carnal fashion when that worldly and carnal fashion *does* offend weaker people, an offense that is called a sin against Christ. Undoubtedly, this sin against the weak consciences of others, which is a sin against Christ, will one day be the very reason for wood, hay and stubble being burned up at the Judgment Seat of Christ.

The inescapable conclusion to the entire issue is that modesty and gender-distinction not only involves misunderstood and misapplied Bible verses, but it is also the unmentionable abomination in too many fundamentalist circles. Too many pastors have shied away from this issue because they do not want to "risk the ire" of certain folks who do not want to give an honest consideration to one of God's unchanged commands.

Furthermore, these pastors do not wish to lose their marvelous statistics by having folks leave the church over the issue. The inescapable conclusion is that several Bible colleges and Christian camps have abandoned what they call "legalistic dress codes" because they do not want to alienate modernists and lose the support base they need to maintain their state-of-the-art campuses and campgrounds. The inescapable conclusion is that a majority of believing parents have shied away from this issue in the name of "choosing their battles." Not wanting to deal with what they consider a small issue, they actually allow the very thing that will lead to bigger battles.

To those who have reneged on their responsibility on this issue yet call themselves by the separatist title or the independent Baptist name, there is a need for careful, compassionate and clear preaching on this issue. It is the telling of a sad tale when a guest in an independent Baptist church can see that the only modesty and gender-appropriateness in the church is in people over age sixty! It is the swan song of separatism when gender-indistinction and immodesty become more and more tolerated in the pews because those who sit in the pews today vote for the next pastor ten years down the road.

The inescapable conclusion is that most persons born since 1960 have no concept of a culture in which ladies looked modest and acted like ladies. Sadder still is the inescapable conclusion that most believers alive today have no concept of a church in which ladies in general display discreet chastity, modesty and holy femininity. Consequently, many of those women miss being treated with due respect and singular honor.

Twisted femininity, called feminism, is not as distasteful today as it was even twenty years ago. This hyped-up philosophy, whose spokespersons are the likes of Jane Fonda and Hillary Clinton, is a base system of ideas whose main goal is "equal rights" for men and women but whose end result is women who get treated like the lowest of men. Where were wife-beating, divorce, homelessness, abortion and a score of other scourges of women prior to 1960? They were nearly unheard of. Equal rights and immodest, manly dress have hurt womanhood. Most people do not treat ill-attired women in the same way they treat a woman who looks like a lady.

Another inescapable conclusion is that most persons born since 1960 have no concept of a culture in which men looked and acted like men, in which men displayed a godly masculinity and in which men in general were gentle, kind, loving and peaceful. The inescapable conclusion is that most believers alive today have no concept of a church in which men dress up for God and stand out in their culture as men of God. Therefore, the present-day twisted masculinity called machoism is much less abominable today than it was at its inception. Machoism is a hyped-up philosophy whose spokespersons are sports idols and Hollywood whoremongers whose goal is personal gratification at the expense of the purity of women. Much of this personal gratification is the ability to have a woman to escort whose shape is displayed through form-fitting clothing.

Biblical manhood would never expose a woman to the gawking of boorish men on the streets, in the businesses and at every place of entertainment. Questionable indeed is the quality of Christianity of a man who approves of his wife or daughter exposing her body to the entire world, either through lack of clothing or through form-fitting, contour-conformed, immodest, gender-blended clothing.

In short, those who seek in any manner to ignore this oft-misunderstood concept of modesty and distinction are turning away their ears from hearing God's commands, and yes, much more than commands. God has also spoken on the subjects of modesty and gender distinction in His Law, His testimonies, His precepts, His statutes, His judgments and His ways. How pertinent, then, is God's proverbial wisdom:

"They that forsake the law praise the wicked: but such as keep the law contend with them.

"Evil men understand not judgment: but they that seek the LORD understand all things."

"He that turneth away his ear from hearing the law, even his prayer shall be abomination.

"Whoso causeth the righteous to go astray in an evil way, he shall fall himself into his own pit: but the upright shall have good things in possession."—Prov. 28:4, 5, 9, 10.

Modern man has chosen to disregard all this. Independent Baptist fundamentalists in increasing numbers are disregarding all this. Biblical Christians must not let men's shoutings obscure God's still, small voice. The Scriptures of God always commend modesty, chastity, propriety and singularity of the attire for males and females, men and women, boys and girls. Biblical charity always takes the higher road, always embraces the holier, the godlier, the purer and the better. Biblical liberty always lives by the rule of refusal to offend, which is the rule of stricter standards, not looser ones.

Gender differences are created differences and are to be displayed by the two genders in every way. Since there is nothing that displays a person any more than his clothing, perhaps some readers will take notice and stop sliding by on this one and get back to chaste gender distinction that really says to the world around us, *I belong to Jesus Christ and I am not ashamed of my distinct appearance, even though it is not stylish or fashionable or accepted in this day and age.*

One of Dr. Tom Malone's famous statements was this:

"Separation is to our salvation what
sterilization is to an operation."

The separation of biblical Christians from the admittedly alluring and provocative clothing styles of the world would sterilize their testimonies and clean up a whole lot of infection.

chapter five

The Three E's: Education, Entertainment, Employment

Fundamental-ish Learning and Living

Scripture says, "As he thinketh in his heart, so is he" (Prov. 23:7). Scripture does *not* say, "As a man believeth in his heart, so is he." That is the reason another verse says, "Keep thy heart with all diligence, for out of it are the issues of life" (Prov. 4:23).

The man who believes the five fundamentals, but *thinks* like the emergent church leaders or the Rick Warren crowd or the Neo-Evangelical will actually *behave* like their thinking style in short order. Regardless of belief, God clearly reveals that a man behaves in accord with his thinking and choosing processes.

This is not a semantic corn maze dreamed up to add another chapter to a book. This is a realistic issue that must be addressed. When a man believes all five fundamentals but allows himself to think upon compromise as tolerable, he will eventually admire compromise. His behavior will reflect his thinking, even if he attends a church with a really good doctrinal statement of belief and even though he says he believes all those sound doctrines.

Thinking comes from a variety of sources, but without even the possibility of doubt, the main influences upon twenty-first-century thought in the United States are the education institutions, the entertainment industry and the employment establishment. For this reason, as "evil men and seducers...wax worse and worse, deceiving and being deceived" by humanism (II Tim. 3:13), godly men and believers must wax stronger and wiser, instructing and being grounded in truth. All the bellyaching about narrow-mindedness among independent Baptists and all the ballyhooing about open-mindedness among the "informed crowd" creates in the modern believer's experience an appetite that cannot be righteously satisfied.

Quite to the contrary of what some men in the ministry seem to believe, when Paul said, "Give attendance to reading" (I Tim. 4:13), he was not referencing Bible commentaries or devotional books. He was admonishing Timothy to give attendance to reading the Bible! Any preacher who invests less than a simple majority of his reading time to the study of the Bible is cheating himself and those to whom he ministers. Believers who do not devote themselves unselfishly to the reading of Scripture are cheating themselves and the family members for whom they hold responsibility.

The foolish idea that one must know everything that is going on in the world if he is to be effective needs to be exposed. For all but the last fifty years, mankind functioned within extremely small spheres of influence and awareness. Christianity did not die out in some places because of lack of knowledge of what was happening on the other side of the world. Instead, miracles and revivals happened!

That children are to be educated is a given; regardless of whether a culture is pagan or Christian, poor or wealthy, indigenous or multi-ethnic, rural or urban, the parents pass down information and skills to their children. Call it education, call it training or you may call it bestowal of a heritage. Call it what one will—it is the parents and grandparents who play the role of teachers while the children are the learners. In the nation at large, there exists a wide array of educational philosophies and an accompanying broad selection of educational methods.

It is the common Neo-Evangelical philosophy to infiltrate; therefore, their method of education follows suit, in that the vast majority of New Evangelical families help to populate the facilities of public education from preschool to post-graduate programs. Some of the boldest and loudest spokespeople championing the infiltrative educational philosophy among New Evangelicals are sponsoring grassroots moves to "take back the schools for God" and "get the Bible and prayer" back into the schools. Their advocacy for re-introducing Deity, requiring discipline and restoring decency is admirable at the social level. However, the education of one's children is hardly limited to the social stratum of one's life.

Education is supreme, sacred and spiritual! While it is true that many religious organizations claim that the Bible is their ultimate rule for faith and practice, their support for the United States education system, entertainment monstrosity and employment philosophy defies this claim. The tenets of biblical faith are mocked and denied by schools that are tax-funded, by media that is anti-God and by employers who are motivated by greed.

education

The boundaries of biblical practice are ridiculed and broken by the secular state-financed institutions of higher learning. From the earliest pre-K programs to the doctoral level, the National Education Association (reportedly one of the nation's largest unions) supports atheism, paganism, agnosticism, pluralism, heathenism, humanism and a dozen other -isms; however, that same NEA refuses equal time and place for biblical Christianity. In fact, the NEA proudly subscribes to the Humanist Manifesto and just as proudly advertises its overt hatred of biblical Christianity.

Because of the dearth of biblical faith and practice in schools at every level, the New Evangelical push to infiltrate looks and sounds quite logical—even spiritually sensible. However, the laws of the physical world teach that once a squash has rotted, it cannot be restored to prime edible soundness to be baked for Thanksgiving dinner. Just as surely, the spiritual and moral decay of the nation's schools is incurable and reminiscent of Isaiah's words: "...the whole head is sick, and the whole heart faint. From the sole of the foot even unto the head there is no soundness in it; but wounds, and bruises, and putrifying sores: they have not been closed, neither bound up, neither mollified with ointment" (1:5, 6).

Consider what would happen if pragmatists were successful in "taking back the schools." One of the first issues to be addressed would be the god to whom they would pray. Who would it be? Allah on Monday. Native American spirits on Tuesday. Buddha on Wednesday. The saints on Thursday. Jehovah on Friday. The students would hear the name of Jesus only as often as they heard the name of Vishnu, Confucius, Hare Krishna, the Dalai Lama, the Pope, Buddha, Mohammed and a host of other messianic imposters.

Another of the issues to be handled if the compromising crowd were able to "get God back into the schools" would be the holy writings that would be read. The children in the classrooms could hear the Bible only as often as they could also hear the Torah, the Koran, the writings of Joseph Smith, Mary Baker Eddy, Charles Taze Russell, Buddha and a score of other false prophets. Also, when the Bible was read, what Bible might it be that the tolerant inclusivists would use to introduce the public-school students to their concept of God? The NIV, the ESV, the Queen James (the Queen James Bible is an edited version of the KJB, in which all references to homosexuality have been edited so as not to offend homosexuals), or the New Revised this or that version? Obviously, in the interests of multiculturalism and nondiscrimination, all of them in their contradictory confusion would have to have a hearing—all of them except the King James Bible, that is.

Another issue to be addressed in this infiltration-modification effort to take back the schools would be the personnel to whom would fall the duty of teaching the students. Once again, compromise and toleration would dictate that teachers could be pagan or religious (but not decidedly scriptural), immoral or amoral (but not outspokenly moral), asexual or bisexual or transsexual or homosexual (but not avowedly gender-specific by Creation), adulterating or fornicating or experimenting (but not clearly pro-traditional marriage/family), pro-abortion or pro-choice (but not pro-life), evolution-tolerant (but not Creation-tolerant), and so on. The fabric of the faculty would have to be woven with broad stripes of the inclusivist cloth.

Finally, if this open-mindedness can overtake the schools, the decision of what is taught must be made. In honor of infiltration and tolerance, the curriculum would include humanism with some Christian terminology, evolution with a few theistic overtones, liberty of personal expression with the occasional moral decoration, religion with both cultic and occult exposure and socialization with the occasional restriction.

All of this flies in the face of God, who commanded Jeremiah the prophet to tell His people, "Thus saith the LORD, Learn not the way of the heathen" (Jer. 10:2). Again, Solomon commanded, "Cease, my son, to hear the instruction that causeth to err from the words of knowledge" (Prov. 19:27). Biblical Christians cannot walk together with such perverted thinking when God has made such statements through His Spirit-anointed Bible writers. The error of educational inclusivism is the exposure of the children to the learning of the world. God told His nation,

> "When thou art come into the land which the LORD thy God giveth thee, thou shalt not learn to do after the abominations of those nations.
>
> "That they teach you not to do after all their abominations, which they have done unto their gods; so should ye sin against the LORD your God."—Deut. 18:9; 20:18.

Independent Baptist fundamentalist pastors who do not speak boldly of the evils of the pagan public-school system, along with the parents who thrust their children—innocent and naive—into this cesspool of perverted, anti-God thought are creating a ghastly problem for the generation that will populate independent Baptist churches in the next twenty years.

What this denial of separation and embrace of humanism is accomplishing is akin to what occurred in Israel as is recorded in Psalm 106:35, where God stated that His people "were mingled among the heathen, and learned their works." The drastic consequences of that mingling and learning are listed in ensuing verses in that Psalm: serving and being snared by the idols of their culture (vs. 36), sacrificing their sons and daughters to devils (vss. 37, 38), sullying their own works with the ideas of their day (vs. 39) and soliciting the anger of the God of Heaven against themselves to the degree that they lost their freedoms (vss. 40, 41).

One cannot help but observe that the formerly Christian United States has indeed come into the precarious position of threat by immoral perverts and radical religionists. This has all developed since the embrace by believers of the unbelieving agenda of public education. Truly, if the saints of God do not make a drastic U-turn, God may once again give His people over to the tyranny of the heathen, the haters of God and the hand of oppression.

The sister epistles of Ephesians and Colossians give but brief instruction to parents. Both epistles could have given a lengthy list of all the things parents ought to do, but the single instruction is for fathers (and by marital association, mothers) to rear their children "in the nurture and admonition of the Lord" (Ephesians 6:4). In the contexts of both Books, this instruction is presented as the opposite of or the cure for provoking children to wrath and discouragement.

There exists—admittedly for good reason—the argument that "Moses was learned in all the wisdom of the Egyptians" (Acts 7:22) and that in spite of having been trained in such paganism "was mighty in words and in deeds" and "when he was come to years…[chose] rather to suffer affliction with the people of God than to enjoy the pleasures of sin for a season" (Heb. 11:24, 25). For this isolated reason alone, modern reasoning puts children in public schools to "be witnesses to the pagans."

Statistically, however, the number of those who end up serving God as Moses did rank among an infinitesimally small minority. Furthermore, it must be remembered that it was not Jochebed's faithful teaching but the humanistic and pagan teaching of Pharaoh's daughter that taught Moses that the way to solve a dispute was by murder! Just so, a staggeringly tragic percentage of "Christian" children who graduate from the public schools today do so with a sad resume of spiritual shipwreck, moral defilement, humanistic influence, carnal motivation, materialistic enticement, emotional discouragement and inner bitterness.

Independent Baptist fundamentalists who follow biblical Christianity cannot walk together in dialogue, devotion or dependence with the current trends on the subject of the educating of children, because biblical Christians have boundaries. Biblical Christians must be the teachers.

Biblical Christianity must be the main subject and the foundation of all curriculum. The students must be from biblical Christian families who are willing—yes, insistent—that their children be taught God's truth to the total and absolute exclusion of man's philosophies. The independent Baptists cannot walk together in the direction of anti-biblical thought trends and cannot walk together for the distance of the years throughout their education, because fundamentalists are not pressing toward the same educational destination that inclusivist, eclectic pagans are pursuing.

entertainment

Beyond the churning oceans of post-modern pagan education lie the utterly disastrous waters of the techno-entertainment industry. Casual reading of the Book of Acts will not uncover a church consumed by entertainment but will reveal believers praying, reading Scripture and testifying of Christ. The believers of the first century made an impact upon culture. This is quite different from the believers of the twenty-first century, who are being impacted by culture.

Again, this same search in the pastoral epistles will fail to offer pastoral instructions on the entertainment of the congregation. Further, church epistles will give no space to the church's pursuits of entertainment. Even the carnal church at Corinth was praised for its gifted leaders and members but had no room for any positive reference to entertainment for believers. Perhaps the church of this century should examine some historical times when entertainment was the focus.

One such time transpired in the days of Isaiah who addressed the Jews and specifically the inhabitants of Jerusalem as "thou that art full of stirs, a tumultuous city, a joyous city." He continued by stating that the dead of the city of Jerusalem were "not slain with the sword, nor dead in battle" (22:2). The word "stirs" refers to clamorous unrests and continuous riots. This city of Jerusalem, which had once been the glorious capital city of the united Israel, had become an idolatrous and capricious city full of tumult and danger; however, the dead were not dead on battlefields. Rather, the "dead" of Jerusalem were the dead who "lived" in apathy. In the hearing of the citizens of that once-great city, God had called for "weeping... mourning... baldness, and...girding with sackcloth." Instead, the entertainment-crazed Hebrews went blindly forward with their "joy and gladness, slaying oxen, and killing sheep, eating flesh, and drinking wine." (Isaiah 22:13)

Their entire focus was "let us eat and drink; for to morrow we die" (vss. 12, 13). Indeed, this city that was called tumultuous and joyous in one breath showed itself to be a city given over to the worldly happiness that disregards holiness. Sadly, the Lord told His people they would "not be purged from" this sin until their death (vs. 14).

Continuing his strain of prophecy against the people who held holiness in contempt and considered happiness to be their ultimate end, Isaiah addressed Shebna who was over the house and asked him why he had hewed out a sepulchre when he was never going to need it. The reason he would not need it is that Jerusalem would be taken captive. In that day Eliakim would be enthroned and the key of David would be committed to him. All Judah would depend upon Eliakim and "hang upon him all the glory of his father's house." Unfortunately, because the people would persist in their carnal, worldly pursuit of entertainment and despise repentance and restoration, "the nail that [was] fastened in the sure place [would] be removed, and be cut down, and fall and the burden that was upon it [would] be cut off" (vss. 24, 25).

The prophet Ezekiel, ministering generations later, encountered the same preoccupation with entertainment. Even though by his time, the Babylonian captivity had occurred and the chastening of the Lord had been severely felt, the Jews in Babylon had not learned to put faith ahead of fun nor righteousness ahead of revelry. God spoke to His faithful prophet and said,

> *"Also, thou son of man, the children of thy people still are talking against thee by the walls and in the doors of the houses, and speak on to another, every one to his brother, saying, Come, I pray you, and hear what is the word that cometh forth from the LORD.*
>
> *"And they come unto thee as the people cometh, and they sit before thee as my people, and they hear my words, but they will not do them: for with their mouth they shew much love, but their heart goeth after their covetousness.*
>
> *"And, lo, thou art unto them as a very lovely song of one that hath a pleasant voice, and can play well on an instrument: for they hear thy words, but they do them not."*—Ezek. 33:30–32.

Aside from the music and modesty of true Baptist fundamentalism is the methodology of true Baptist fundamentalism. Methods are perhaps more subjective than music or modesty; however, there are enough clear guidelines in the Word of God to give churches, church leaders and church families both wisdom and practicality in the how-to area of ministry.

Attrition due to spiritual apostasy, moral atrocity and civil anarchy is causing membership and attendance numbers to dip to frighteningly low points. Consequentially a large number of churches have resorted to an entertainment-centered ministry in order to attract people back to their churches.

Like many cultures in the past, the present-day society of the United States of America is obsessed with recreation. People who will not drive to church two miles from home if there are six snowflakes in the air will risk life and limb to drive their child to an away basketball game on icy roads with whiteout blizzard conditions. People who find it painful to part with a five-dollar bill in a church collection plate will pay exorbitant fees for center-court basketball tickets, rink-side hockey tickets and fifty-yard-line football tickets. People who claim to be too busy to attend even one weekly church service find time to attend several athletic practices and games in the same week if their children are involved.

Beyond the athletic realm are the incidents of vacationing and traveling. With the national calendar of the United States already sporting New Year's Day, President's Day, Easter, Mother's Day, Father's Day, Independence Day, Labor Day, Columbus Day, Thanksgiving Day, and Christmas Day—and with many of these now providing three- or four-day weekends—the call for travel gets louder. Combine that with fractured and distributed families and the church ministries stand to suffer damage at least one weekend out of nearly every month of the year.

Vacationing and traveling are right in their place, even as any recreation is right in its place. The key is "in its place," but a suitcase-happy culture has found that "out of town" is also a convenient way to be "out of church."

Again, the lust for pleasure and recreation broadens to include games and hobbies at every age level. Once, in this land hobbies were for old men and women who had worked hard until age seventy and had earned the privilege of "enjoying retirement." Today's culture is beset with a generation that expects the pleasures of retirement every weekend of the year to the careless neglect—if not the arrogant disdain—of worship of service to the great God of Heaven.

This all boils down to a narcissistic pursuit of weekly, if not daily, self-gratification and momentary gaiety that is as fundamental to the fabric of the twenty-first-century family and community as colors are to a rainbow.

One response to this has been to make church entertaining. Beginning in the second half of the twentieth century, Neo-Evangelicalism filtered its way into large numbers of mainstream churches and transformed what were once churches that embraced the five fundamentals of the faith into socially progressive and spiritually regressive centers of a newly-defined worship.

Sunday school underwent a slow mutation from being an hour of biblical instruction to being ten minutes of Bible story time followed by fifty minutes of craft-making and game-playing. Focusing upon the experience and satisfaction of the parishioners as opposed to the exaltation and service of Christ, the leaders of this movement turned church services into everything from staid, liturgical tombs to chaotic circuses.

Independent Baptists looked on in horror because the dialogue of entertainment church did not fit with the conversation of independent Baptist Christianity. Devotion to fun and games did not coincide with devotion to the church and the Christ who died for her. Dependence upon the emotional highs of edge-of-the-seat entertainment did not parallel dependence upon the Holy Spirit and the resurrected Christ for spiritual victory. The direction in which one traveled to have fun was entirely different from the direction one pursued to know God. The distance that new-agers and fun-worshipers could travel with independent Baptist Bible-believing Christians was only a short hop here or there, because the destination of the former was the next cutting-edge thrill while the destination of the latter was triumph over Satan, crucifixion with Christ against the world and the flesh and true power against temptations and sin.

employment

The matter of employment must be approached carefully. The author knows that believers are responsible to pay their bills and that bill-payment comes through employment. The author knows that there are, for a wide variety of causes, single-parent homes, and that the single parent must have a job. The author knows that economic highs and lows in the various regions of this large nation dictate high and low economic times in homes and families. The author knows that there will be occasional situations where an unavoidable circumstance hinders the Christian. And finally, this author knows that independent Baptists who live in those regions where the economy is weak must tighten their belts and sacrifice.

However, the independent Baptist separatist movement used to be supported by laborers who set aside Sunday as the Lord's Day. In the giving of the Ten Commandments in Exodus, chapter 20 and in Deuteronomy, chapter 5, more space is given to the Fourth Commandment than is given to any other single commandment.

Shockingly, more space is given to the Fourth Commandment in each of these passages than is given to the Fifth through the Tenth Commandments combined! The worship day was to be guarded strictly.

When the Lord Jesus Christ rose from the dead on the first day of the week, He met with His followers both morning and evening on that first day. It is a safe assumption that He met with them every first day of the week after that, until His ascension from Bethany, recorded by Luke in Luke 24:50 and 51 and in Acts 1:1–9. The worship day was not "done away" with, as liberal and Neo-Evangelical writers would have us believe. The worship day was not designated as "personal choice" as the false Christian liberty movement would have us believe. The worship day was not relegated to "just another day" as disobedient believers and agnostics and atheists would have us believe. No, not at all. The worship day was simply changed to our weekday known as Sunday, the first day of the week, in honor of Jesus Christ's resurrection and ascension.

A careful study of Hebrews chapters 3 and 4 renders a simple verdict: the believer's rest is connected to his observance of the Lord's Day. Hebrews 3:7, 8 implore the New Testament believer to hearken, not harden.

Following is a passage of exhortative warning regarding Old Testament believers who did not enter into a restful life of faith. Believers are admonished to use caution "lest there be in any of you an evil heart of unbelief, in departing from the living God" and "lest any of you be hardened through the deceitfulness of sin." What more graphic way is there to demonstrate departure from God and hardness of heart than to use Sunday as a workday instead of a worship day?

Chapter four of Hebrews starts with an encouragement to

fear the Lord and not fall short of entering His rest. The text of chapter four addresses Creation rest which was one day out of seven and Canaan rest which was one day out of seven as well as one year out of seven. Then, Hebrews 4:9–11 tell the New Testament believer:

> *"There remaineth therefore a rest to the people of God.*
>
> *"For he that is entered into his rest, he also hath ceased from his own works, as God did from his.*
>
> *"Let us labour therefore to enter into that rest, lest any man fall after the same example of unbelief."*

Following that is a great passage on God's Word and prayer, the two primary components of public worship of Jesus Christ.

Sunday ought to be given to the Lord Jesus Christ from the moment of rising to the moment of reclining.

Sunday should not be a day of gainful employment any more than it should be a day of gaiety and extravagance. It ought to be the Lord's Day, given to Bible study, prayer, singing, worshiping, serving and helping. It ought to be the Lord's Day given to loving God with heart, soul, mind and strength. It ought to be the Lord's Day, given to loving neighbor as self. It ought to be the Lord's Day, period.

A majority of independent Baptists are not even mentioning this anymore! It is complacently accepted that a sizeable portion of the church's workforce will be out of the pew either Sunday morning or Sunday evening or both. It is complacently accepted that faithfulness is "just not possible" any more, that believers' service to Jesus Christ must revolve at some comfortable distance around their pursuit of vocational success, material gain and personal fulfillment. Work too often has become god to too many.

There is tragic credibility to the statement that, in the United States, "We worship at our work, we work at our play, and we play at our worship."

The great crusade by independent Baptists to serve God wholeheartedly on Sunday and work the other six days has been all but abandoned.

It is one law and "whosoever shall keep the whole law, and yet offend in one point, he is guilty of all" (Jas. 2:10). The great fight to maintain the display of the Ten Commandments in public places is weakened by independent Baptists who offend in the one point of disregarding the Lord's Day. The tragic consequence of disregard of the Lord's Day has brought shameful statistics to independent Baptist families in the areas of divorce, waywardness and bankruptcy.

May God give back to us a generation of God-fearing souls who will trust God and pray mightily for His supply in spite of the cultural disdain for a day of worship. May God give us saints who would be thrown to a burning fiery furnace before they would bow to the idol of today's Nebuchadnezzar-like, anti-Jesus-Christ and pro-pagan-religion world of employment.

In conclusion of this chapter, let the men and women of independent fundamental Baptist churches band together to educate both adolescents and adults in the holy truths of God. Let the men and women of independent fundamental Baptist churches band together to pray and trust God for employment and career pursuits that allow for Sunday to be the Lord's Day all day.

chapter six

What Has Happened to All the Churches?

The Rise of the Fundamental-ish Church

With even a casual consultation it is easy to see that both Corinthian epistles were addressed "unto the church of God which is at Corinth" (I Cor. 1:2; II Cor. 2:1). Galatians was sent "unto the churches of Galatia" (Gal. 1:2). The Thessalonian epistles were written "unto the church of the Thessalonians which is in God the Father and in the Lord Jesus Christ" (I Thess. 1:1) and "unto the church of the Thessalonians in God our Father and the Lord Jesus Christ" (II Thess. 1:1).

Multiple references in Acts and the epistles mention "the church which was at or in Jerusalem" (Acts 8:1; 11:22); "the church that was at Antioch (Acts 13:1); "the church which is at Cenchrea" (Rom. 16:1); "the church that is in their house" (Acts 16:5; I Cor. 16:19); "the church of God" (I Cor. 10:32; 11:22); "the church which is in his house" (Col. 4:15); "the church of the Laodiceans" (Col. 4:16; Rev. 3:14); "the church that is at Babylon" (I Pet. 5:13); "the church of Ephesus" (Rev. 2:1); "the church in Smyrna" (2:8); "the church in Pergamos" (2:12); "the church in Thyatira" (2:18); "the church in Sardis" (3:1); "the church in Philadelphia" (3:7); and "the church of the Laodiceans" (3:14).

What, then, is the contemporary anathema about the word *church?* What is happening these days to the churches? All one need do is peruse internet websites or the yellow pages under the heading *Churches* to find out that many of what used to be called churches are now called worship centers, family ministries, Christian aid centers, community evangelical chapels, new life fellowships, and other such names. Some of these locations of supposed worship of the true God of the Bible have resorted to calling themselves names that seem both outlandish in claim and nebulous in meaning, such as The Rock Church, The River of Life, The Potter's House, Church of the Stone or Messiah Fellowship. The incidence of these alternate names for *church* increases with each new day, while the number that still uses that holy and biblical title *church* decreases.

To be sure, the words *chapel, ministry, center,* and *fellowship,* are not bad words. Neither is the word *church* a bad word. Notably and interestingly, in Scripture the Lord named His called-out assemblies churches. Not one of the epistles is addressed to the Christian center at such and such a city, the ministry in this or that location, the Fellowship at Brother So-and-So's house or the streams of water in whomever's house.

In the New Testament the words *chapel* and *center* do not exist. The word *ministry,* as used in Scripture, means either a positional office within the sphere of the local church or the general service of God, usually with an emphasis upon the Word of God; however, this word is never used to denote the called-out assembly of the saints or the building where that called-out assembly assembles. The Bible word *fellowship* is used as a synonym for unhindered communion with God or with the saints or as a general term for common characteristics between two different individuals or parties; never in the New Testament is this word employed to name the local congregation of saints or its meeting place.

Let it be clear that, while this is not a censure of every local assembly that has a name other than *church*, this is a notation that God used the word *church* and did not use the other words to speak of the location where believers gather in a local assembly for worship and service. And lest one split semantic hairs about whether the church is a building or the people in the building, let us at once remember that the English language employs other words that simultaneously refer to buildings and to the people who gather in them. *School* is one such word. When someone says, "Let's go to the school to watch the band practice," the person is referring to the building and its location. However, when someone says, "Our school is playing its biggest rival in the home game tonight," the obvious reference is not to the building or even its location, but to the students who are playing a game at some location—perhaps the school but maybe a local park or stadium—against other students. The question remains—what is happening to the churches?

One thing that is happening to churches is that they are disappearing because of the spiritual stigma in a post-modern, pagan culture which does not like the word *church*. The very presence of that word strikes at the heart of antagonistic atheism and apathetic agnosticism. The word *church* is simply and undeniably incompatible with modern culture. Therefore, to avoid what is considered a negative association, a spiritual reproach or even a cultural stereotype of a church, some religious organizations are abandoning the word altogether. Many of these groups have gone to greater lengths, removing crosses and other symbols from their letterheads, signs and buildings. Steeples are either pulled down or never erected. The building styles are altogether those of gymnasiums or arenas, so that the ministry or center may have more of a visible testimony as a hub of activity than as a holy sanctuary.

A second thing that is happening to churches is a national doctrinal decay whereby churches are being renamed because of the definitive doctrine associated with the name *church*. As "the house of God, which is the church of the living God, the pillar and ground of the truth" (I Tim. 3:15), the church is to be the bastion and bulwark of biblical belief, the castle of Christian creed, the fortress of the faith and the headquarters for the heralding of the Gospel! Not wanting to be identified with doctrine, many religious organizations are withdrawing from the title *church* and settling upon inclusive, inviting, innocuous names.

Many of today's worshipers, opting for a religious experience that caters to feelings, have left the churches where they heard the Gospel of Jesus Christ and were delivered from the flames of Hell in favor of a soft-pedaled, nicey-nice, come-as-you-are place where nobody believes much or expects anything.

A third thing happening to churches is satanic interference, the spiritual battle being waged between the forces of Jesus Christ and the forces of Satan. The less frequently society encounters Bible words, the happier the Devil is. The less often children growing up hear the word *church,* the more often the tempter rejoices. Sadly, in the name of relevance and keeping with the times, many who have at least a semblance of spiritual desire are distancing themselves from churches, preferring association and affiliation with nondenominational, interdenominational and Neo-Evangelical bodies that bear little resemblance to the true church of the living God!

Most Americans who "go to church" do not go to a biblical,

New Testament church. The abandonment of the purity of the New Testament church has been followed by the allurements of the Corinthian/Laodicean church, which results in the removal of the candlestick and the absence of the New Testament church. The physical building often remains in use long after the spiritual purpose has disappeared, the spiritual preacher has moved on and the spiritual people have died (either spiritually or physically).

In the absence of the New Testament church, all manner of organizations have arisen: Big Brothers Big Sisters, Boys Clubs, Girls Clubs, Boy Scouts, Girl Scouts, public schools, and yes, organizations that are called churches but are not. Some people want to keep the idea of church alive in their minds because of the comfort that word brings them; they do not, however, want to keep New Testament ideas in mind because of the discomfort those ideas would bring them. Therefore, they call what they have and do "church" even though it is no more church than an aardvark is an automobile.

Another thing happening to churches is derived from the trendy, "out-with-the-old-and-in-with-the-new" mentality that discards any and all that can be considered passé or irrelevant in favor of that which is perceived as cutting-edge. Observing, as they do, that church attendance is falling across the board and across the nation, these groups decide to title their buildings and organizations using words that "draw a crowd" rather than "drive the crowd away." Alexander Pope said something like, "Be thou not the first by whom the new is tried, nor be thou the last by whom the old is cast aside." When presented with the opportunity to have over five thousand disciples instead of His meager twelve, the Lord Jesus preached "a hard saying" (John 6:60), and "from that time many of his disciples went back, and walked no more with him" (vs. 66). Apparently, the Lord Jesus was not relevance-motivated. He obviously valued a few holy, dedicated disciples over thousands of bread-seekers.

A fifth thing happening to churches is that leadership boards of some religious organizations are aware that their organizations really are not churches. Rather than engage in false advertising, they call themselves by names that are more accurate. In such cases, the boards in charge ought to be applauded for honesty, but they should take their candidness a step farther and inform their Sunday—and their Saturday night—crowds that they have not attended church but rather have experienced an emotional pep rally where everyone wears a steeple-shaped hat for good luck.

While it is true that these things already mentioned are happening to churches, the thing happening to churches that is pertinent to this publication is the overall fundamentalist faltering. Presented already as five-point fundamentalism, this faltering has contributed to an erosion of once valuable and sacred separations. The balance of this chapter addresses several areas that, while they may not merit an entire chapter, are specific to the subject and pertinent in independent Baptist circles.

PASTORS AND INFLUENCE. Preachers within the ranks of fundamentalism possess not only the *responsibility* to call their congregants back to God, but also the *influence*. When independent Baptist pastors decide to pursue the five-point mindset, they bear enormous responsibility. The prophet Jeremiah thundered against watering down in Jeremiah 23:22. In context, of course, he was exposing the false prophets who told the Jews who were facing imminent judgment, "Ye shall have peace," and "No evil shall come upon you" (vs. 17). However, as Jeremiah continued in this strain, he brought to light a most regrettable truth: that if the prophets had stood for God's truth and preached that truth to the people, the people would have turned from their evil way (vs. 22). How tragic! How calamitous!

If only the prophets of Judah had done in Judah what Jonah did in Nineveh! But they did not.

By application, then, independent Baptist pastors who do not stand up and stand out beyond the five-points of 1930s fundamentalism are, in some measure, responsible for the embracing of worldly ways by members of their congregations! James' solemn warning of teachers receiving a stricter judgment than hearers comes to mind (Jas. 3:1). Jesus' profound statement that more is asked from those to whom much is committed arises in one's thoughts (Luke 12:48). Jeremiah's stringent conclusion that breaking off the yokes of wood results in the forging of yokes of iron enters one's conscious meditation (Jer. 28:13).

consider these thoughts:

1) James solemnly warned that teachers would receive a stricter judgment than hearers (Jas. 1:3).

2) Jesus stated profoundly that more is asked from those to whom much is committed. (Luke 12:48).

3) Jeremiah stringently concluded that breaking off the yokes of wood results in the forging of yokes of iron. (Jer. 28:13).

The process by which a church moves from strong, biblical, independent Baptist fundamentalism to five-point fundamentalism to New Evangelicalism is subtle in process and may be either slow and steady or sudden in progress. When a man who is the leader of a church hedges and hesitates on separation in one or two areas, he opens a Pandora's box he can almost never close. A weak stance on one issue leads to another because the people who were drawn to his church by his first olive branch of pacification are always weaker still than he is; they will undoubtedly request and even demand his neutrality on some other issue. Refusal of their expectation ensures that they will leave his church; their leaving his church will stifle the impressive statistics and hinder the growth climb. His only option is crumbling on yet another area of separation.

THE PROCESS CONTINUES. Each subsequent erosion of separation makes his church attractive to yet weaker and weaker believers and to greater numbers of unbelievers, who then make more demands for more placation. Eventually, compromised beyond what he can stand, the pastor is "led to move on to another church." Now with a sizeable minority or even majority of worldlings, what kind of pastor does this congregation call? You guessed it. That group will appoint as their leader a puppet who is neither-nor instead of either-or in his positions. The church, once a beacon of light, a city on a hill that could not be hid, is now a flickering candle, one of a thousand buildings in a skyline, indiscernible, undetectable and irreparable.

PASTORS AND EXAMPLE. Independent Baptist pastors also have a role in setting an example which they expect followers to follow. After all, what good is an example but to be followed? With all respect to the gray-headed and very aged men of our movement, some of them have weakened due to their declining health and waning acuity. They themselves never listened to rock music, nor did they ever have rock music in their homes; however, they won't stop it from being used at youth outings. Their wives and daughters never dressed in skimpy, gender-neutral, skintight clothing; however, they don't address the issue when church leaders allow their wives and daughters to dress that way. They themselves never watched in their homes the media that is inappropriate due to blasphemous conversation and sexual innuendo; however, they have long since stopped preaching about this problem.

Some of these fundamentalists resemble King Saul's footmen in I Samuel 22:17–19. They themselves would not carry out the carnage of slaying the Lord's priests and their families and their city, but neither would they step in to stop Doeg from killing them. King Saul's footmen should have stepped up and prevented this senseless slaughter just as they defended Jonathan when he tasted the honey in the day of battle. Indeed,

> *"If thou faint in the day of adversity, thy strength is small.*
>
> *"If thou forbear to deliver them that are drawn unto death, and those that are ready to be slain;*
>
> *"If thou sayest, Behold, we knew it not; doth not he that pondereth the heart consider it? and he that keepeth thy soul, doth not he know it? and shall not he render to every man according to his works?"*—Prov. 24:10–12.

Five-point fundamentalist preachers and parents who back down on one or two areas are paving the way for the next generation to be drawn to the death of sacred Bible truths. God will render to them according to their tranquilized pacification.

PASTORS AND ACCOUNTABILITY. Independent Baptist pastors, thirdly, have grave accountability to stand at all the battle fronts, not merely in the "big battles." Again, the sagacious words of Jeremiah cross the centuries and bear up-to-date weight, as if he were the featured speaker at this year's major preaching conference! Listen to him: "If thou hast run with the footmen, and they have wearied thee, then how canst thou contend with horses? and if in the land of peace, wherein thou trustedst, they wearied thee, then how wilt thou do in the swelling of Jordan?" (Jer. 12:5).

The soul-searching questions of the prophet's sermon on the broken covenant should penetrate all independent fundamentalist consciences with unabating conviction. He who does not stand in the small issues will not stand in the big issues. He who dares not in the seemingly trifling matters will not dare in the big matters.

Independent Baptist fundamentalists who are wearied running with the footmen of adulterers soon fall behind the galloping steeds of sodomy. Five-point fundamentalists who are wearied running with the footmen of marriages between the godly and the ungodly soon eat the dust of the chariot horses of divorce and repeat marriages. Compromising fundamentalists who are wearied running with the footmen of edgy entertainment are soon overtaken by the speedy steeds of pornography. Hedging fundamentalists who are wearied running with the footmen of ministry politics soon find themselves trampled underfoot by the horses of corrupt leadership. Baptist fundamentalists who are wearied in the land of peace regarding gender-distinct clothing will drown in the flood of unisex tolerances. Those who are wearied in the land of peace concerning compromising musicians will drown in the flood of compromising preachers. Any who are wearied in the land of peace touching literal, six-twenty-four-hour-day creationism will drown in the flood of evolutionary tolerances. All who are wearied in the land of peace pertaining to any spiritual, moral or ethical issue will drown when Jordan overflows its banks.

PASTORS AND CHURCH ITSELF. Fourthly, independent Baptist pastors have a mandate to make church church again. The idolatry of "fun" has crept in and overrun many a ministry. Every Sunday's excitement threshold has to be higher than the excitement threshold of the Sunday before. The stimulation factor of every youth outing has to trump the stimulation factor of the previous youth gathering. The thrill at each college-career function has to outdo the thrill of the last college-career get-together. Everyone has to be sure that everyone has fun at church and church functions. This is a perspective on fun, not a tirade against it. Paul's pastoral instruction to Timothy, Titus and Philemon is devoid of instruction about the church members having fun. These pastoral epistles, written so that pastors would know how to behave in God's house (I Tim. 3:15), do, however, instruct "that the aged men be sober…the aged women likewise… the young women to be sober… Young men likewise…In all things shewing…a pattern of good works: in doctrine shewing uncorruptness, gravity, sincerity, Sound speech that cannot be condemned…" (Titus 2:2–8, selected).

The Book of Acts (which we fundamentalists say is the pattern for our churches) is empty when one begins looking for ways the first-century Christians had fun. To the believers of the New Testament age, the new life in Jesus Christ was a battle, not a game—a cause, not a competition with a championship—and armor, not costumes. Victory was measured, not in points, but in Holy Spirit power and resurrection power.

This author is supportive of family reunions for birthdays and other commemorative occasions, of holiday celebrations (be they patriotic or symbolic) and of sporting events for the sports' sakes. However, these must be subject to the greater good of the work of Jesus Christ. The reason that Paul never instructed his preacher boys and that Acts never mentions fun is not that first-century believers never had fun. Rather, the absence of mention in Scripture of saints having fun is due to the fact it was so insignificant it did not bear mention in the holy writ. For that reason, among many, fun in God's house needs to be stringently limited and church needs to be church again. Revival—national, local or personal—never occurs while people are having fun. Revival ensues when church is church, when saints are sober-minded, when believers are teary-eyed, when prayers are cried out, songs are sung out and the Devil is driven out.

PASTORS AND EDUCATION. Independent Baptist pastors must return to the cry for biblical, scriptural, Christian education of the children within their churches. With the halcyon days of the Christian education movement behind us and the horrific days of the pagan education movement upon us, it behooves us to realize the will of God on this matter, that being that God "will have all men to be saved, and to come unto the knowledge of the truth" (I Tim. 2:4). Biblical fundamentalists are doing quite well on the saved part, but in the coming-to-the-knowledge-of-the-truth part, more and more within the churches of independent Baptist fundamentalism are relying upon the world for the education of their children!

Regrettably, the knowledge to which children and adolescents are coming in this day's education system is the knowledge of pagan lasciviousness and post-modern licentiousness and perverted lies. There is no truth in the history class, because the history has been rewritten to exalt rebels and extinguish patriots. There is no truth in the science class, because science has been rewritten to establish evolutionism and destroy creationism. There is no truth in the "social studies" classes, because social studies have been rewritten to accommodate psychology and psychiatry and debunk salvation. There is no truth in the physical education class, because the entire curriculum of sports has been rewritten to elevate physical fitness and promote sexual freedom but mock gender distinction and morality and innocence.

Finally, independent Baptist pastors within the ranks of fundamentalism must observe the process that takes a church from being church to being something other than church. First, there is elasticity, a stretching of long-respected, long-observed biblical boundary lines. This usually takes place under the guise of staying relevant when more concern needs to be placed upon staying reverent. After elasticity comes complicity, a cooperation with others who stretch different long-respected, long-observed biblical boundary lines. This happens when Pastor A puts up with Pastor B's stretch if Pastor B will shut up about Pastor A's stretch.

Following the elasticity and the complicity is the complexity. Read a dress code for a Christian summer camp in 1970 and the same camp's dress code for today. If that camp has stayed true, the elasticity and the complicity of pastors require the camp directors to write up a complex dress code, a complex "what-not-to-bring-to-camp list, a complex unacceptable behavior list, a complex unacceptable language list, etc. In order to cover everything that has to be addressed, the camp brochure has to be many pages long!

Read the handbook of a Christian college from 1970 and then read their handbook for today. If that college has remained faithful to the Word of God, the same situation has developed. The handbook is a thick drudgery of rules and regulations that would be completely unnecessary if the teens and twenty-somethings who enroll in said colleges were as Christian in their sanctification as they insist they are in their salvation.

What comes after this complexity? Sadly, futility. Pastors and evangelists, Christian college presidents and Christian camp directors, parents and grandparents—too many become discouraged with the fight and become convinced that it is futile to try to be godly because that just "drives people away."

What is next? The final result of all this is that people are saying, "I don't know what a Christian is, but I think I am one." After all the elasticity, complicity, complexity and futility comes apostasy.

Apostasy may come quickly and directly like someone driving I-90 from Chicago to Boston. Apostasy may come slowly and indirectly like someone else driving I-90 from Chicago to Seattle, then I-5 from Seattle to Los Angeles, then I-10 from Los Angeles to Jacksonville, and then I-95 from Jacksonville to Boston. Boston is still the destination regardless of the route traveled.

Regardless of the underlying cause for the dissolution of the Baptist fundamental distinctions of any local assembly, Christians must resist the modern siren songs that lure unsuspecting believers toward the reefs of tolerance, ambiguity and blendedness. In mythology, the sirens were half-woman, half-bird creatures who sang to sailors on the sea. Rather than warn sailors of impending danger and doom, however, the sirens were sisters who sang from beyond impassible reefs and wooed sailors to their deaths. Their songs were so sweet and their draw so strong that sailors would forget even to eat. Some would perish from starvation while the survivors would press on toward the music and wreck their ships on rocky shoals and die. Jason, the reputed captain of the mythological ship *Argo*, was thus tempted. Odysseus, another character of mythology, knew the irresistible power of enticement of the sirens and filled his sailors' ears with wax so they could not hear the dangerous melodies that would spell doom to all. Orpheus, yet another of mythology's legendary characters, drew his lyre and played music louder and more lovely than even the sirens could produce, thus sparing sailors in their temptation.

And something very similar has happened to many of the churches.

Would to God that a generation of God-fearing, whole-Bible-believing, Christ-honoring, Holy-Spirit-filled, independent Baptist fundamentalists would fill their ears with the truth to drown out the sound of the sirens' call for pragmatic modernization of the church. Would to God this generation of godly, holy, separated men and women and children would play the music of the true church so loudly and beautifully that the sirens' music would not only sound sour and flat but would be irgnored altogether.

Thus, the generations to come would have at their disposal churches—true churches—where they might worship and serve their blessed Creator Savior. May God grant us, as true independent Baptist fundamentalists, the acuity and perception to see this trend, stop it in our own lives and churches, preach against it and stand against it! May God grant us an army of preachers who will stop de-savoring the salt, stop dirtying the water, stop diluting the truth and stop dimming the light! May God help independent Baptist fundamentalists get back on board with God about our charity and liberty, our music, our clothing, our polity, our schooling, our recreation and our work! May the God of the true church indeed enable us in these last days to remain truly fundamental in our independent Baptist beliefs, and may he prevent us from settling for the mediocrity of being fundamental-ish.

SWORD OF THE LORD
PUBLISHERS

Publishing the World's Finest Christian Literature

swordofthelord.com